Pisces

Pisces

FEBRUARY 20–MARCH 20

*Your Sun-and-Moon Guide
to Love and Life*

Ronnie Dreyer

Ariel Books

**Andrews McMeel
Publishing**

Kansas City

For information write Andrews McMeel Publishing, an Andrews McMeel Universal company, 4520 Main Street, Kansas City, Missouri 64111.

www.andrewsmcmeel.com

Interior artwork by Robyn Officer

ISBN: 0-8362-3563-0

Library of Congress Catalog Card Number: 97-71538

Contents

Contents

Contents

Contents

Pisces

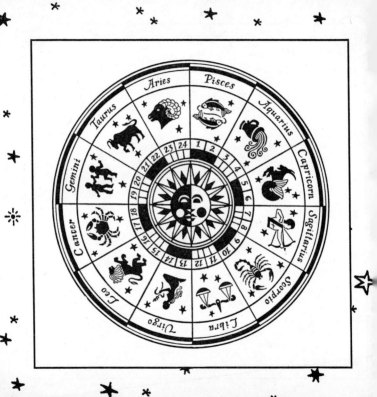

Introduction

How, *you ask, might* astrology make a difference in your life, in your mental, emotional, and spiritual growth? Of course, there is no single answer to this question, for the responses are as diverse as humanity itself. Some of us may wish to dabble, enjoying astrology as we would a new hobby; have some fun; check out our sign and the signs of our friends, lovers, and children; and muse over the romantic possibilities of various combinations. What, for example, are the chances that a Libra man and a Pisces woman would hit it off? Others of us might wish to embark on a lifelong adventure, plumbing the depths of esoteric wisdom and emerging with startling new revelations about ourselves and our lives. Whatever your interest, you will find that astrology has something for everyone.

Astrology, which began as a search for a pattern in the cosmos, is based on the relationship between the infinitely large and the infinitely small, between the macrocosm—primarily our solar system, with its Sun, Moon, and planets, but also the fixed stars beyond—and the microcosm, the mysterious individual personality. In other words, astrology is the study of how celestial bodies influence the Earth and affect the human beings who dwell here.

In this regard, it's important to understand that astrology deals with symbols. The signs of the zodiac represent powerful forces, profound energies of the mind, heart, and soul. These energies are expressed in our personal horoscope, or birth chart, which describes the position of the heavens at our moment of birth and therefore portrays our unique personalities, our likes and dislikes, our strengths and weaknesses, our hopes and fears.

A horoscope is not, however, a simple reading of the future, a trip to the fortune-teller. You might want to consider your horoscope as a kind of map, indicating, say, the model of car you are driving, the condition of its motor, the state of the road (which may be bumpy in some places and smooth in others), and the variety of spiritual and emotional terrain you are likely to encounter during your life's journey. Perhaps the motor needs a tune-up; perhaps two roads pass through a particular stretch of wilderness, one road potholed and poor, the other sure and clear; perhaps just off the beaten path lies a great marvel you would miss if you didn't know it was there. What you do with the map astrology provides is up to you: You are free to choose, free to act as you will, free to make the most of your life—and, too, free to have plenty of fun along the way.

A Brief History

Long ago, men and women looked up into the starry night sky and wondered what it was and what effect it had on their lives. From that first primordial inquiry, astrology was born. No one quite knows how far back astrology's oral tradition extends; its first appearance in recorded history dates to 2500 B.C. in ancient Mesopotamia, where it was believed that the heavenly bodies were great gods with powers to influence the course of human affairs. Those early astrologers began to observe the heavens carefully and keep systematic records of what they saw in the great glittering silence of the night sky. The royal family's astrological counselors advised them on how to rule; early in its history, astrology was considered the "royal art."

The ancient Greeks already boasted

an ample pantheon of gods by the time
their astronomers began to use the new
science of geometry to explain the work-
ings of the heavens. The Greeks com-
bined Mesopotamia's form of astrological
divination with their own mythology and
the new science of geometry, developing
a personal astrology based on the zodiac—from the Greek *zodiakos kyklos*, or
"circle of animals"—a belt extending
nine degrees on either side of the eclip-

tic, the Sun's apparent annual path across the sky. The belt was divided into segments named after animals—the Ram, the Bull, the Crab—and set to correspond to certain dates of the year. The Greeks were thus able to use astrology to counsel individuals who were curious about the effect of the heavens on their lives; the art of reading personal horoscopes was born.

As one seer of the times said, speaking of the heavens, "There is no speech nor language where their voice is not heard." Astrology was incorporated into Roman culture and spread with the extension of the Roman Empire throughout Europe. With the rise of Christianity, astrology faced a challenge: After all, it seemed to suggest that humans were determined by the stars, rather than by the stars' creator, who also, according to emerging Christian theology, had granted humans free will. Generally, however, astrology was absorbed into Christian teachings and continued to flourish; witness the selection of an astrological date for Christmas. Like much of classical culture, astrology went into decline during the Middle Ages, emerging in the early Renaissance to occupy a privileged place in the world of learning; in the sixteenth and seventeenth centuries, it was embraced by the prominent astronomers

Tycho Brahe and Johannes Kepler and was taught as a science in Europe's great universities.

Eventually, the discoveries of modern science began to erode the widely held belief in astrology's absolute scientific veracity. In our times, though, astrology remains as popular as ever, as an alternative to scientific theory, and as a way for people to articulate the manifold richness of the self. Psychologist Carl

Jung noted that astrology "contains all the wisdom of antiquity"; for modern men and women in search of the soul, it holds perennial interest as an expression of the psyche's mysterious relationship to the myriad wonders of the universe.

The Heavens

An Overview

In *astrology, the art of* relating events on Earth to influences in the heavens, each celestial body exerts its own form of power, which is modified according to its geometric relationship with the others. The heavens are made up of several kinds of celestial bodies. First, of course, there is the solar system—the Sun, Moon, and planets. Beyond the solar system lies the infinity of fixed stars, so-called because, as opposed to the planets, which the ancients could observe moving across the sky, the stars were always in the same place. Your horoscope plots the placement of the celestial bodies at the time of your birth.

When we speak of the heavens in astrology, we often speak of the zodiac, an imaginary belt extending nine degrees on either side of the ecliptic, the apparent path of the Sun across the sky. (Remember that the zodiac was devised in antiquity, when it was believed that the Sun revolved around the Earth.) The zodiac is divided into twelve arcs, or constellations, of thirty degrees each. Each arc is accorded a name and associated with the dates during which the Sun made its annual passage through that region of the sky at the time the zodiac was first devised. Your sun sign, the most widely known of the many astrological signs, refers to the particular arc of the zodiac through which the Sun was passing at the time of your birth. (With the procession of the equinoxes, the solar path may not always correspond to the actual solar chart.) The zodiac belt also contains the orbits of the Moon and most of the planets.

The solar system, then, constitutes the most important influence on human affairs. In ancient times, it was believed that the planets had their own light (the Sun and Moon were considered planets). Only five planets—Mercury, Venus, Mars, Jupiter, and Saturn—were visible to the ancients; Uranus, Neptune, and Pluto have been discovered over the last two hundred years. The influence of each planet depends on its position in the zodiac and its relation to the other celestial bodies, including the fixed stars. While some astrologers maintain that the planets are primarily refractors of influences from the more distant stars, most believe that each planet, along with the Sun and Moon, has its own characteristics that uniquely influence us—how we think, feel, and act. This influence can be positive and constructive or negative and self-destructive. Ultimately, the planets' disposition in your chart is a way of expressing various possibilities, which you can interpret and act upon as you choose.

The Solar System

Most astrologers
agree that the primary

influences come from within our own solar system—the Sun, Moon, and planets. Each planet is said to rule over one or two signs of the zodiac and have sway over a particular part of the body. Over the centuries, each planet has come to represent or influence a different aspect of the personality.

The Sun, which rules Leo, represents the conscious, creative aspects of the self. In a chart, a well-placed, strong

Sun indicates a dignified, self-possessed, affectionate, and authoritative personality; a badly placed Sun can suggest an ostentatious and dictatorial nature. The Sun rules the heart. Solar types tend to be energetic (the Sun, after all, is our source of energy) and like to take on large-scale projects that make good use of their many talents. They often make excellent top-level executives.

On the other hand, the Moon,

which rules over zodiacal Cancer, represents the imagination and is often linked by astrologers with the unconscious, hidden part of humans. In a chart, a prominent Moon usually indicates a sensitive and vulnerable nature, which can often be quite delightful; a badly placed Moon, however, can suggest an unhealthy and even dangerous self-absorption. In terms of the body, the Moon rules over the breasts. Lunarians are adaptable and often protective; perfectly capable of enjoying the delights of a quiet life at home, many also seek the public spotlight.

Mercury, the smallest planet and the one closest to the Sun, rules Gemini and Virgo. Like the Roman messenger of the gods whose name it shares, Mercury represents communication, speech, and wit, along with an often changeable disposition. Mercurians tend to be sensitive to their environment; they epitomize verbal and written expression and are often journalists and writers.

Venus, the most brilliant planet, rules Taurus and Libra; the planet of love, it governs the higher emotions, physical beauty, creativity, sex appeal, and sensual experience in all its many forms. It has rule over the throat. Venusians love beauty and art; they can at times be concerned with the surface of things, allowing image to become everything.

Mars, the planet that physically most resembles Earth, rules over Aries; representing the physical side of life, it combines with Venus to influence our sex drive. In a chart, Mars means courage, confidence, and the aggressive urges— the result-oriented ability to take on a project and get it done. In terms of the body, Mars has sway over the sex organs, particularly for men.

Jupiter, the largest planet in the solar

system, rules Sagittarius and represents the more profound realms of thinking and mental life, as well as the depths of the spirit. Jupiter suggests generosity, loyalty, success, and steady, solid growth. In terms of the body, it has sway over the thighs, liver, and blood. Jupiterians tend to be thoughtful, even philosophical, with plenty of social skills and an adventurous love of travel; Jupiter women are often strikingly beautiful.

Saturn, the farthest from Earth of the traditional planets, represents fears, uncertainties, and materialistic concerns. It can indicate practicality, patience, and honesty, although, if badly placed in a chart, Saturn can also suggest a deep fear of life. It governs the human skeleton, emphasizing this planet's role in providing structure and control; Saturnians tend to make good accountants and bureaucrats.

Uranus, discovered in the eighteenth century, rules Aquarius. Often representing change, even upheaval, it can be a beneficent influence, representing the kind of brilliant flash of insight that can instigate bold new ways of thinking. Yet its independent and rebellious nature can pose problems, when liberty turns to license and at times even to crime.

Neptune, discovered in the mid-nineteenth century, has rule over Pisces.

On its beneficent side, it can represent idealism, art, and imagination; its connection with the sea (Neptune was the Roman god of the ocean) indicates its tendency to affect the unconscious aspects of the psyche. This can bring great power; it can also, however, suggest a preference to dream rather than act.

Pluto, discovered in 1930, now rules Scorpio. The planet farthest from the Sun, Pluto often represents the dark forces of desire and instinct that seek dissolution of the self within the great cosmos. While there are dangers here, there is as well the potential for profound healing.

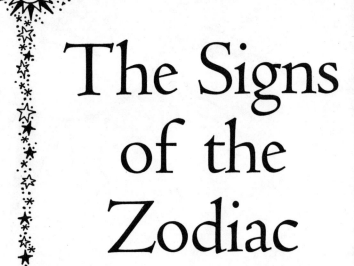

The Signs of the Zodiac

*W*hen we speak
of the signs of the zodiac,

we refer to the twelve thirty-degree arcs of the sky into which the zodiac is divided. Each sign is represented by an image derived from ancient descriptions of the constellations; however, the astrological signs of the zodiac should not be confused with the actual constellations whose names they sometimes share. The most important signs are the sun signs, by which is meant the particular zone of the sky through which the Sun was passing at the time of someone's birth.

The signs of the zodiac are as follows:

Aries (the Ram), March 21–April 20

Taurus (the Bull), April 21–May 21

Gemini (the Twins), May 22–June 21

Cancer (the Crab), June 22–July 23

Leo (the Lion), July 24–August 23

Virgo (the Virgin), August 24–September 23

Libra (the Scales), September 24–October 23

Scorpio (the Scorpion), October 24–November 22

Sagittarius (the Archer), November 23–December 21

Capricorn (the Goat), December 22–January 20

Aquarius (the Water Bearer), January 21–February 19

Pisces (the Fish), February 20–March 20

The zodiacal signs are also symbols for the great forces that lie deeply within our minds, hearts, and souls and exist in different combinations from one person to the next. Each sign is associated with a different part of the body. In total, the twelve signs express all that we are as humans. The signs are said to be composed of four different elements and three different qualities.

The Four Elements

The *four elements* through which the twelve signs of the zodiac are expressed are fire, earth, air, and water. For the Greeks, they were the fundamental substances of the universe. In astrology, these elements are also spiritual and symbolic; they are expressed in connection with three different qualities—cardinal, fixed, and mutable. Each element has one cardinal sign, one fixed sign, and one mutable sign; and each quality is expressed through each element, as in the chart that follows:

	Cardinal	*Fixed*	*Mutable*
Fire	Aries	Leo	Sagittarius
Earth	Capricorn	Taurus	Virgo
Air	Libra	Aquarius	Gemini
Water	Cancer	Scorpio	Pisces

In addition, the four elements, which are restless and in conflict with one another, are often said to be bound together by a mysterious, invisible fifth element, known as the "quintessence," which is responsible for maintaining the often tenuous unity of all things on Earth.

Fire Signs

*T*he fire element, expressed through Aries, Leo, and Sagittarius, is profoundly linked to the spirit. Fire is a powerful elemental force; impulsive, iconoclastic, and warm, the fire signs are eternally seeking expression. If not regulated in some way, however, fire can turn destructive, burning out of control.

Aries—outgoing, idealistic, enthusiastic—requires great freedom in order to achieve its maximum sense of self. Often brimming with confidence, the Aries type tends to act impulsively and not always with proper concern for what other people may think or feel. This spontaneity can be tremendously attractive, but it can at times become selfish and over-bearing.

Leo, on the other hand, while also possessing a deep need for freedom, tends to be much more sensitive to others. Given to the exuberant and flamboyant, Leo's creativity is frequently expressed through art and drama. Self-reliant and generally optimistic, the Leo nature also has a vein of altruism; Leos can, though, at times be a bit vain.

Sagittarius, the mutable fire sign, is characterized by qualities of profound yearning and aspiration. Open, honest, and generous, Sagittarians tend to be hungry for growth and expansion. They are very independent—sometimes to a fault—and are often great seekers, for whom the journey is more important than the destination.

Earth Signs

*T*he earth element, expressed through Taurus, Virgo, and Capricorn, is deeply connected to physical things. Generally, it reflects the practical, down-to-earth side of human nature. It is also said to be an incarnating principle by which spirituality takes on form. Not surprisingly, the earth and water elements enjoy a close relationship, with earth stabilizing water and water making the arid earth fertile.

Taurus, the fixed earth sign, tends toward the sedentary. Slow, practical, and conservative, a person born under Taurus will likely evidence an unspectacular, solid determination. Taurus is receptive to the joys of a gentle, stable existence—a regular paycheck, a nice house, warm relationships, a comfortable routine. When frustrated or threatened, however, the Taurus nature can turn possessive and jealous.

Virgo, the mutable earth element, is drawn toward ephemeral things, engrossed in "what is past, or passing, or to come." Intellectual, elegant, intelligent, and methodical, Virgo is driven to seek the clarity of understanding. When subjected to intense stress, though, Virgo can become hypercritical and a bit of a nag.

Capricorn, the cardinal earth element, is dependable, solid, trustworthy, and prudent. The Capricorn nature will plow steadily ahead, connected to its roots and clear about what it wishes to achieve in life. Yet in stressful situations Capricorn can become selfish and rigid.

Air Signs

The air element, expressed through Gemini, Libra, and Aquarius, has long been associated with thought, dating back to the ancient concept that thinking is the process by which humans take in ideas from the world around them, much as they take in air through breathing. All three air signs generally are dominated by tendencies toward restlessness; they are also known as the nervous signs. However, they are each unique.

Gemini is particularly volatile, a whirlwind constantly blowing in many directions. The Gemini nature is inventive, alert, and communicative, but Geminis can at times become unstable and wild, even hysterical.

Libra is like a strong wind that blows purposefully in a single direction. Its influence is elegant and orderly. Libras tend to be perceptive and affectionate, sensitive to others and aware of their needs, although in excess a Libra nature can be impractical and a bit lazy.

Aquarius, the calmest air sign, is associated with water as well as air; it represents spiritual knowledge, creativity, and freedom. The Aquarian nature tends toward the rational and places great value on freedom, sometimes sacrificing the future in the name of rebellion.

Water Signs

The water element, expressed through Cancer, Pisces, and Scorpio, represents the fluidity, spirituality, and sensitivity in our nature. Often emotional, sometimes to the point of instability, the water element needs to find some kind of container in order to realize its true potential.

Cancer, represented by the Crab, is emotional, imaginative, and romantic; it can also be very cautious. There is something gentle and shy about the Cancer nature; afraid of being hurt, it is sometimes slow to come out of—and quick to return to—its shell. Such vulnerability can be deeply touching; in excess, however, it can turn moody and self-absorbed.

Scorpio, the most self-confident of the water signs, is masterful, shrewd, and determined. Possessed of strong desires, Scorpio types are not easily dissuaded from pursuing their goals. In doing so, they can be forceful and inspirational; yet when threatened, they can exhibit a violent streak, and when thwarted they can turn sarcastic and cruel.

Emotional and highly intuitive Pisces is also quick to retreat from the slings and arrows of life. Often this is because the Pisces nature is so sensitive to the emotional needs of others that it will sometimes forget its own interests and need to seek temporary refuge, in order to find its own center again. It has to be careful, though, not to fall into the trap of self-pity.

The Three Qualities

There are three quali-ties, or modes of expression, through which each of the four elements finds ex-pression in the twelve signs of the zo-diac: cardinality, fixity, and mutability.

The qualities are another way of expressing features the different signs share; all four fixed signs, for example, will have certain features in common, in that they will tend to be more stable than the mutable signs within their same element. This may seem complicated, but the basic principle is actually pretty simple.

The cardinal quality serves as the origin of action, the wellspring of energy that gets things done in the world. It's the "mover and shaker" personality—active, outward-looking, more geared to "doing" than to "being." The four cardinal signs are Aries, Cancer, Libra, and Capricorn; each is self-assertive, but in a unique way. Capricorn, the earth cardinal sign, tends to take solid, dependable action that is often geared toward material success, while Aries, the fire sign, often acts in a much more spontaneous, even impulsive, way. Libra, the air sign, is particularly assertive on the intellectual level, quick to advance its ideas and defend them when they are questioned. Cancer, the water sign, tends toward caution and often will act prudently.

The fixed quality serves to temper movement; it functions as an impediment, an often valuable check on the rampant free flow of energy. Sometimes expressed as "will," the fixed signs—Taurus, Leo, Scorpio, and Aquarius—are likely to be resistant to change and appreciate tradition and known, sure values. Taurus, the earth sign, is the most sedentary of all, with deep, latent powers and a clear preference for staying in one place. Leo, the fire sign, embodies a sustained emotional warmth and loyalty that is not likely to change over time. With Scorpio, the water sign, power takes on a more fluid form, exhibiting an unshakable self-confidence that remains firm in the face of adversity. Aquarius, meanwhile, is the most cool and composed of the air signs; Aquarians trust rational thinking and extend deep roots into the ideas they hold and the places where they live.

The mutable quality embodies the principles of flexibility and adaptability. The mutable signs—Gemini, Virgo, Sagittarius, and Pisces—could be said to combine aspects of cardinal impulsiveness with those of the unyielding fixed temperament. Gemini, the mutable air sign, is particularly given to surprising transformations of the self; you think you know a Gemini, and then, *presto!* you realize that you knew only one side of the person's nature. Virgo, the earth sign, is often irresistibly drawn toward the shifting play of ideas and thought. For Sagittarius, the fire sign, change often equals growth; driven to expand, the Sagittarian nature seems eternally questing after something new. Pisces, the water sign, often embodies the fluid, changing character of the emotions; sensitive to the smallest alterations of feelings, it can ride the waves of emotional life like a skilled surfer.

Pisces

An Introduction

P*isces, the twelfth sign* of the zodiac, is ruled by the planet Neptune and symbolized by the Fish. As the final sign in the zodiac's great wheel, Pisces in some way sums up all the preceding signs and represents death, rebirth, and reincarnation. This is the sign of eternity.

Pisceans are the most mystically minded of all the signs; you inhabit Neptune's great ocean, which in astrology represents emotions, the unconscious, the intuitive powers, and the world of dreams. Most Fish live in the changing world of feelings, as you'd expect of a sign of the mutable quality and the water element. Natives of this sign tend to have a dreamy quality; you're rarely ambitious and generally don't plan for the future, preferring to swim along through life, letting your intuitions be your guide. You often seem to pursue your own inner world rather than worldly riches; preferring the watery depths of your own dreams, you can, when faced with adversity, be prone to self-deception. Most of you Fish are deeply spiritual and blessed with a marvelous imagination that particularly favors music and art. In general, you possess a wisdom as deep and myste-

rious as the ocean itself, and it's not unusual for Piscean natives to be born with
the gift of prophecy.

The glyph, or written symbol, for
Pisces depicts two fish tied together. It also
represents the human feet, the part of the
body ruled by Pisces. Some astrologers
believe that the glyph also represents
two crescent moons linked by a straight
line, symbolizing the connection between
emotions and the material world.

Myths
and
Legends

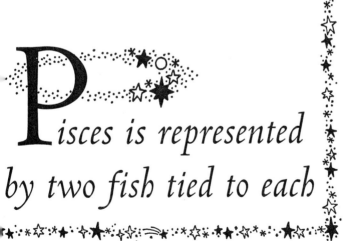

Pisces is represented
by two fish tied to each

other and swimming in opposite directions, symbolizing the psyche's hidden depths and conflicting currents of desire and feeling.

The constellation of Pisces has long been linked to images of fish. Babylonian astrologers named this constellation Kun, which means "tail" as well as "leash." The fish symbolized two fish goddesses named Anunitum and Simmah (representing the Tigris and Euphrates Rivers) who were tied together. The fish also appear in a story in Greek mythology. According to legend, one day a many-headed monster named Typhon threatened Venus and her son, Cupid, who were out for a stroll along the banks of the Euphrates. The terrified Venus, goddess of beauty, implored her father, Jupiter, to save her from this terrible monster. In response, two brave fish jumped out of the river, took the imperiled goddess and her son on their backs, and plunged back into the water, carrying them to safety. In honor of their bravery, the two fish were raised up into the heavens, where they became the constellation Pisces.

In early Christian times, the fish, symbolizing Christ, was also linked to the Pisces constellation, as well as to the Greek fish goddess Atargatis. In those days, Pisces was under the influence of Poseidon, the Greek god of the sea. Back then, in traditional astrology, Pisces was ruled by the planet Jupiter, named for the most powerful god in Roman mythology. When the planet Neptune was discovered in 1846, it displaced Jupiter's rulership, and in modern times Pisces has been under Neptune's sway. Named for the Roman god of the ocean, Neptune is the planet of imagination, idealism, illusion, and deception. Many of you Fish, of course, possess these traits in abundance.

Neptune has also been said to facilitate contact with the great sea of the unconscious; it should come as no surprise, therefore, that many of you Pisceans are deeply in touch with the latent powers of the psyche, and you are naturally attracted to the truly profound mysteries of life. Few signs can rival the expansiveness of your imagination—indeed you are one of the most creative signs. But sometimes this trait works against you because you have a tendency to escape into your private world of dreams rather than face reality head-on.

Symbols
and
Associations

The symbol of the
two fish tied together

and swimming in opposite directions perfectly expresses the essence of your nature. You swim through life, carried by occasionally shifting currents of feeling and often contradictory desires. You live in your feelings and can be given to extremes of temperament. You are the dreamer of the zodiac and you are hardly ever practical or logical.

The cord linking the fish has been called the Silver Cord and has been said to represent the subtle and mysterious power that holds together the human spirit and soul. Pisces is the sign of spirituality, but you usually keep your spiritual side hidden to the world, because you are more comfortable that way. You do try to nurture your soul, whether that means going to a house of worship or taking meditative hikes in the woods.

In terms of the body, Pisces rules the feet. Your special colors are green and turquoise, the colors of the sea. If you were born between February 20 and February 28, your birthstone is the amethyst. If you were born between March 1 and March 20, your birthstone is the aquamarine. Another gemstone associated with Pisces is the pearl. Your lucky day is Friday and your lucky numbers are two and six. The cities ruled by Pisces are Lisbon, Casablanca, Alexandria, Dublin, and Seville—all but the last being seaside cities—while your countries and regions are Portugal and, surprisingly, the great Sahara Desert. Your plants are the poppy, the water lily, and other water plants, as well as willow and fig trees. Your metal is platinum. And in the animal kingdom, of course, Pisces rules fish and dolphins.

Key words associated over the centuries with the positive side of your nature include *poetic, sentimental, mystical, compassionate, understanding, imaginative, romantic, gentle, kind,* and *sympathetic*. Negative attributes and associations, on the other hand, include *impractical, lazy, unstable, hypochondriac, fickle, escapist, self-pitying,* and *overly dependent*.

The list of famous Fish testifies to the sign's creative, imaginative, and emotionally rich nature. Polish composer Frédéric Chopin, whose music ranks with the most emotionally pure of all time, was a Fish, as was the great sculptor

Michelangelo. Such writers as novelist Lawrence Durrell, diarist Anaïs Nin, poet Elizabeth Barrett Browning, and the French Romantic novelist/poet Victor Hugo all explored in their own way the complexities of the human heart. Other great Piscean artists and writers include dancer Rudolf Nureyev, painter Piet Mondrian, writers John Steinbeck and John Updike, opera singer Enrico Caruso, and actress Anna Magnani. With your brilliant minds, Pisces can be great scientists as well, such as Albert Einstein, Nicolaus Copernicus, and Galileo. Fish can even, albeit rarely, be great statesmen, such as George Washington.

Health
and
Physique

While all kinds
of Fish swim in the sea,

many Pisceans share a number of physical attributes. For natives of this sign, perhaps your most important feature is your eyes, which are often sensitive and have a rather sleepy appearance. Generally speaking, you give off a slightly dreamy, otherworldly look, reflecting how your souls are inclined toward the contemplation of a truer kingdom.

Natives of this sign are generally short and stocky with a muscular build.

Male Fish tend to have broad shoulders and a full, rather fleshy face. Female Fish usually have strong upper arms and calves and a heart-shaped face. Females also may have lovely large eyes, a charming soft smile, and smooth clear skin. And, chances are, Female Fish give off an air of feminine mystery that men find extremely attractive.

Many Pisceans appear rather clumsy. It's only natural—with your intense imagination engaged in myriad adventures of the deep, how can you be expected to negotiate easily the trying topography of terra firma? When the Little Mermaid walked on land, after all, did she not feel as if she were walking on knives?

The signs of the zodiac are related to human anatomy, with each sign ruling particular organs and areas of the body. Your sun sign, therefore, can help indicate where you might be vulnerable to illness or injury. Since the feet are ruled by Pisces, you're likely prone to various troubles of the feet and toes, such as bunions, corns, boils, and certain deformities.

Otherwise, your physical health tends to be quite closely connected to your emotional well-being. When you feel loved and happy and have a way to express your dreams, you rarely fall ill.

However, when you feel down—sensing that your dreams are being thwarted—you can be susceptible to various ailments. This can be a real problem because, as a mutable water sign, you're subject to many mood swings and can often find yourself feeling depressed. When this occurs, you have to be particularly careful to avoid excessive drinking or smoking, self-destructive behaviors to which some Pisceans, in time of stress, can be prone. Nevertheless, most Fish live long lives. Although you do not relish sports, you do excel at activities that accentuate your muscular strength, such as weight lifting, rock climbing, and rowing. These pastimes have the added benefit of alleviating your bouts with the blues.

Personality

As the twelfth and final sign in the

zodiac's great wheel, Pisces encapsulates all that has gone before and anticipates all that is to come. What, exactly, does this mean? Simply that the Piscean personality is remarkably rich and complex. Intuitive, dreamlike, compassionate, and profound, Pisceans are often considered the "wise old souls" of the zodiac.

First and foremost, as the mutable water sign, you're deeply in touch with the ever-changing parade of your feelings. Indeed, you live in the great ocean of emotion, upon whose tides you're constantly, if not always easily, adrift. When you're in the sea of feelings, you are really in your element. For many of you Pisceans, these currents of feeling carry you into a wide range of underwater haunts—after all, your symbol is two fish, linked by a cord, swimming in different directions. This reflects the complexities of your nature; you're drawn both to the clarity of the shallower waters and to the brooding mysteries of the deep.

As with anyone open to experiencing fully the life of the emotions, you can at times swim into some troubled waters. You never quite know how you'll be feeling an hour from now, and since you feel things so deeply, hurts that others might shrug off can drive you into a funk, even into a depression. And natives of this sign sometime tend to seek solace from painful realities in the world of dreams.

But then again, your innate capacity to feel life so intensely opens up for you vast domains of experience. You're in all likelihood a kind and gentle soul, remarkably sensitive to the feelings of others. Indeed, you care deeply about those around you and possess an instinctive sense of what might be troubling someone, even when people are unable—or unwilling—to express their feelings. (However, you do have to be careful not to take other people's problems too much to heart.)

When it comes to making decisions, you rely on your intuition rather than on rational thought; this can occasionally get you into hot water, but it can also allow you flashes of insight akin to genius. Your loving and caring nature ensures that you'll try to help out whenever you can. Such actions are infused with a deep altruism, as well as a mystical connection with the wisdom stored in the great un-conscious.

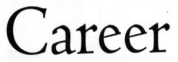

Career

When it comes to your professional life,

you Pisceans tend to wear your feelings on your sleeve. The world of work, in other words, must be a place that appeals to your heart as well as to your bank accounts. Since worldly ambition and the quest for riches likely rank rather low on your list of priorities, you seek out a vocation where you're able to be true to your nature, where you can find genuine fulfillment.

In general, since you prefer work

that offers freedom of expression, you're inclined to avoid cumbersome bureaucracies; you prefer an organizational flexibility that can easily adapt to new situations. You also tend to shy away from strict routines, unless the routine in question corresponds perfectly with the deep-sea rhythms inside you.

So it comes as no surprise that natives of this sign are drawn to jobs in film, television, theater, music, art, and ballet, for you're one of the most creative signs of the zodiac and are always seeking ways to express the richness of feeling that lies within. And with your kindness and compassion, you're also drawn to service professions, where you can help people solve their problems, such as psychology, social work, and various philanthropic causes.

As a general rule (of course, there are always exceptions), you Neptunians rarely find yourselves in executive positions; you're just not driven to climb up the ladder of the organization. However, if you are the boss, you're likely very interested in the well-being of your employees, which can make you a popular and effective manager. Advertising and public relations are two areas where Fish such as yourself can often swim to the top.

If you're an employee, you require

interesting work; otherwise, you can get depressed. A happy Fish is an efficient Fish, but when you feel low, sometimes the quality of your work suffers a bit. With your sensitive nature, the environment in which you work is often particularly important. You need to feel comfortable; this likely means a spacious office, perhaps with plenty of natural light, along with pleasant colleagues. And a job with a casual dress policy, of course, will make you much more happy than one that requires formal business attire. When the space fits and you're able to express yourself freely, you prove a very loyal worker, who, in your own inimitable way, gets the job done.

Love
and
Marriage

*M*atters of the
heart matter more to

you Pisceans than to natives of most other signs. For you, love—in all its forms—is likely the most essential experience of life; indeed, it could be said that, for Fish swimming along in the great sea of feeling, love *is* life itself. Fish are, in other words, the quintessential romantics.

As a result, your relationships tend to be rather intense. As soon as someone awakens the myriad yearnings of your heart, the rest of your life takes a backseat to the all-encompassing trials and tribulations, joys and sorrows, of romance. You easily throw yourself into a new love with a singular kind of enthusiasm and openness. You're usually quite eager to please your new friend; with your sensitivity to the needs of others, you're always on the lookout for new ways to express how much you care.

Of course, you expect your partner to do likewise, and this could mean conflict. Alas, not all of the zodiac's creatures accord love the transcendent importance that you do; you need to be a bit careful not to scare off a more timid soul before the relationship has had a chance to get off the ground. Since you open up your heart so easily and deeply, you can place yourself in a vulnerable position; it's not unusual for you to feel insecure, particularly (but not only) at the beginning of a relationship. As a result, you may find yourself seeking constant reassurance that you are, in fact, loved as much as you love. Again, watch out, lest your new friend find the intensity of your demands too much to bear. There's one other danger as well: Since you tend to retreat into dreams and illusions rather than deal with painful realities, you can sometimes be slow to acknowledge the disturbing fact that a relationship may not be working.

When it comes to sex, most Pisceans

(as a water sign) emphasize emotions rather than the purely physical aspects of desire that, for example, an earth sign might more easily embrace. For you, the physical act of love paraphrases the yearnings of the heart; often physical beauty is less important than emotional kinship. And when you do meet that special someone, you're ready to settle down; after all, it's only natural that true love leads—often quickly—to marriage.

Home
and
Family

With your
legendary interest in

other people, you're ideally suited for family life; indeed, there really is no better way for you to find fulfillment. And as you'd expect of a water sign, your home is as much an emotional place as a physical one. For you, in other words, home is where the heart is.

Your home may or may not be in the best part of town. It may be a grand palace with spacious lawns and towering elms; then again, it could just as well be a small apartment. Since you don't care all that much about money, you may not be able to afford the most posh digs. No matter. What counts is that this is where you live with the people you care about most.

First, your home serves as your anchor amidst the shifting currents of feeling that are constantly carrying you from one mood to another. Here, at last, is a place where you can settle down, where you can love and, most important, feel loved in return. Chances are that your home has a "lived-in" look; you're not exactly the type to keep those protective plastic slips on the sofa and chairs, and there may be no regular cleaning regimen. A bit of untidiness, in fact, doesn't bother you at all—until you suddenly feel anxious about the mess and decide to clean everything up in a whirlwind of energy.

This home is a place where you can

give your imagination full freedom, a place that you can fashion in your own image, transform into a haven of art, music, and other creative delights. You probably have a special space indoors or outdoors that calls to your spirit, somewhere you can write in your journal or sit by yourself quietly. In all likelihood, this household runs on a kind of spontaneous emotional circuitry rather than on rigid rules. Dinner, for example, is prepared when everyone is hungry, not at a set time. You leave your children—and Pisceans love children!—free to pursue their own interests; indeed, you strongly encourage the little ones to revel fully in the endless fictions and fantasies of childhood. It breaks your heart to have to punish anyone; occasionally, you may have to force yourself to impose some measure of discipline. When you do, however, you do it gently, making sure your kids understand what they did wrong. They trust you, knowing that when they're troubled, you'll listen endlessly to their sorrows and concerns. You take great joy in magically making their worries disappear.

Pisces in
Love

Few, *if any,* of the zo- diac's signs attach as much importance to romance as you do. For Pisces natives, emotion equals being: "I feel, therefore I am" is the motto by which you live and by which, in your opinion, everyone else should live as well. From tender affection to flaming passion, all breeds of the magic plant take front stage in the drama of your life. When you're swimming in the great ocean of emotion, you are truly in your element.

When it comes to negotiating the tricky currents of feeling that constitute a romance, few of the zodiac's animals are more practiced than you. With your remarkable sensitivity to the feelings of others, you make a willing and considerate partner. You can be rather insecure; you need to be told that you are loved.

While you can appear quite vulnerable emotionally, however, the experience of being loved brings you great strength and allows you to weather the many stormy seas through which we all must pass.

Since love is so important to you, you're willing to adapt easily to meet the demands of a relationship. (You are, after all, a mutable sign.) Here, though, lies a possible problem: Since you feel that you need love, you will do anything—or almost anything—to keep a relationship alive, even if it means going against your own best interests. But when it comes to the bedroom, Pisces men and women usually make tender and adventurous lovers. For Fish such as yourself, sex is never just sex. It is, rather, an adventure in feeling.

Pisces with Aries

MARCH 21–APRIL 20

Should you hook up
with a Ram, chances are that both of you
will initially think you've found the lover
of your dreams. And who knows? Maybe
you have. Though you share a great deal,

it could be that your confidence in this relationship comes more from how your differences complement one another. In other words, while it may seem that you are at times heading in different directions, you could actually be able to waltz together quite nicely, indeed.

Foremost, perhaps, is the question of your essential natures. The Ram, as the cardinal fire sign, is one of the most aggressive animals in the zodiac; Rams know what they want and don't hesitate to go after it. If your Ram wants you, therefore, he'll let you know. Your imagination and essentially romantic allure will likely light the Ram's fire. And the Ram should be lured by your sense of mystery: Rams are adventurous souls, attracted by the unknown depths that Fish can allow them to understand. You, meanwhile, could easily be drawn by the bold heat of Aries' passion. You'll immediately discover that Rams can be charming; however, as you'll find out, they can prove rather headstrong as well.

As your relationship develops, it'll likely settle into a pattern wherein the bold Ram tends to dominate. In amorous matters, particularly, Rams like to run things. Your Aries lover, therefore, could expect you to adapt to—even, perhaps, to submit in some ways to—his control. "Where are we going to have dinner tonight?" you ask. The Ram will decide, and you will (or should) be thrilled by the choice your new friend has made. In short, if you'll pardon the slightly dated axiom, Rams like to wear the pants in the family.

For some signs this insistence could prove trying, if not downright unacceptable, but your essentially mutable nature often allows you to accommodate such requests without necessarily betraying your inner self. As long as you feel secure with the Ram, little things such as where you're eating dinner won't matter to you. You're quite able to let your stubborn mate have his way, particularly since, in return, your Ram will assure you that you are and will be eternally loved. In short, this is the kind of bargain that could work well for both of you: Your Ram gets a faithful follower, and you get someone you can lean on, who will happily fight your battles, loyally protect you, and generally shower you with affection.

Though it may not always seem so, the Ram does have an emotional side, but you will have to bring it out. This is something you'll do eagerly, since emotional well-being is so important to you. You could easily spend an hour talking about your feelings; the Ram may not contribute that much to the conversation, but at least it will listen to you. Aries, on the other hand, can inject a little practicality into your life, with its down-to-earth ways.

You both can be a little selfish, but when you retire to the bedroom, you'll be happy to find that these tendencies are not, shall we say, set in stone. Indeed, in this regard, anything (or just about anything) goes. After all, you both thrill to the joy of sexual play; come night, you can recover in spades the power that you surrender during the day. Any little spats you may have had can be patched over, and any rough edges smoothed. The Ram's scorching sexual heat combines with your emotional depth to infuse your lovemaking with poignancy as well as passion. Together, you'll play many notes; Aries fire plus Pisces water should cook up plenty of steam.

Pisces with Taurus

At first glance, these two signs may appear to have little in common. After all, you are perhaps the most dreamy and mystical of the zodiac's animals, and the Bull is among the most pragmatic and down-to-earth. You may be surprised to find out, however, that the stars shine favorably on this match: For a number of reasons, there may be a strong attraction between you; while differences do exist, they could prove complementary rather than conflicting. And should problems arise, the chances are good that you'll be able to work through them. All in all, this could be a romance very much worth exploring.

So what brings you, the mutable water sign, together with the Bull, the fixed earth sign? It could well be that old friend, the mystery of sexual attraction. In fact, this affair of the heart could start off with a kind of mute mutual recognition in which you both somehow sense the promise of future ardor. For most Fish, of course, sexual attraction is initially an emotional experience, an expression of your heart's fondest yearning; desire passes through the heart first, then continues on to . . . other places. For many Bulls, desire is often, well, rather more earthy; love develops out of what can at first be a healthy kind of lust. In any case, the upshot of all this is that the Bull can help lend flesh to your feelings, while you can spiritualize the Bull's desire. All in all, not a bad place to begin a romance. One other thing: Most Bulls are by nature quite possessive; though this might drive a Sagittarius crazy, chances are that you don't mind in the slightest. In fact, you may actually like it because it makes you feel secure.

You may quickly discover your conversation is much more expansive than a simple dialogue of bodies. For all its practical sense, the Bull is also deeply artistic, and you'll probably find that you feed off each other's creativity. Look for many museum visits, as well as quiet afternoons and evenings at home, perhaps with you intently working on your writing as your new friend earnestly touches up a painting or two. The Bull's concern with material well-being can also appeal to volatile Fish such as yourself, who are used to drifting with the sea's many changing currents. It might be nice, you begin to think, to drop anchor a bit, let go, and settle in.

Might be nice, indeed. Particularly since the place you'll be settling into is probably not so shabby. (Bulls do like their creature comforts, and as the fixed earth sign, they generally place a higher value—both financial and sentimental—on hearth and home than any other sign.) You could adapt quite easily to a life in the lap of luxury. After a while, though, you may become just a bit bored with all this stability; don't be surprised, therefore, if you occasionally long for the infinite expanses of the wide-open sea. If the two of you can talk it out, however, such regrets should pass, leaving you closer than ever before.

Pisces with Gemini

MAY 22–JUNE 21

When these two mu-
table signs get together, the result can be a
romance as slippery as quicksilver. This
should be fun for a while; you should

171

have plenty to teach each other, and you can be sure that this affair won't be staid and boring. Whether it can last a lifetime is another question.

You can both seem a bit fickle, but you're fickle for slightly different reasons. The Twins are several (at least two, maybe more) distinct selves rolled into a single body; their mutable nature reflects the fact that *they* know who they are. Each self (say, the practical and the romantic) needs proper attention. They're changeable, but they're, in their own way, often self-possessed. And the Twins are rather self-centered as well.

For Fish, however, the reality is somewhat different. Many Fish may not quite know who you are since you identify with your feelings and your feelings are always changing. Adrift on the shifting currents of the great ocean of emotion, you felt one way yesterday; you feel another way today, and, chances are, you'll feel yet different tomorrow. Each feeling, at the moment you experience it, could seem like the "real you."

What can you make of all this? Well, it can mean several things. By your nature, you adapt to the waters in which you find yourself; a relationship means compromise, and you're often willing to adjust to the needs of your mate in return for a sense of security. At the beginning of this relationship, then, you'll likely be willing to accommodate your new friend's constant changes of mood. Complexity, after all, has its appeal, particularly for Pisces such as you, who aren't exactly simple souls. Gemini is ruled by the planet Mercury, named for the ancient messenger of the gods, and is one of the zodiac's most communicative signs. The two of you could indulge in long discussions of your deepest and most complex yearnings. And you're likely lured by your friend's lively wit, which can brighten up even the most serious conversation. In the bedroom, you're compatible enough, although water and air are generally not the sexiest of combinations.

As your relationship progresses, however, your friend's fickleness might begin to wear on you. Since you tend to look to others in order to locate your own center, your sense of self is likely being continually displaced by the Twins' endless vacillation. You might feel that your sensitivity and patience are being abused: While you understand yourself by listening to others, many Geminis try to understand others by listening to themselves. As Gemini's constant prevarications heighten your latent insecurities, you might start clinging and complaining, both of which could threaten the

Twins' need for inner freedom; this air sign, in other words, could get scared of drowning in your watery depths. Finally, at some point, all this could just become too difficult to manage. In spite of the many good feelings you have for each other, you may well, at the end of the day, both prefer to set out for new seas.

Pisces with Cancer

JUNE 22–JULY 23

It *should come as no* surprise that the Crab is among your most compatible partners. Since you're both water signs, you probably place considerable importance on your feelings. In addition to your sensibility, you complement each other in a number of striking ways. When it comes to matters of the heart, of course, nothing is absolutely certain; however, the long-term chances for this love are promising, indeed.

How will you first meet? Perhaps one afternoon you'll head down to the beach to watch the sun set and you'll see that one other person on this isolated stretch of sand is also gazing dreamily into the infinite. Then, quite shyly (Crabs tend to be timid), this person will cast a glance in your direction; suddenly, you'll feel emboldened to stroll over and strike up a conversation. As you gaze into each other's eyes, something very special will happen: It won't be the lightning flash of desire or the warm glow of incipient friendship, but something else, something vaguely spiritual, that will tell you both that you've found a possible soul mate.

The truth is, you share a sensibility. Fish and Crabs both live in an emotional ocean; however, you two make your way through the depths of your feelings in slightly different ways. You, the mutable water sign, are ruled by the planet Neptune, named for the ancient god of the sea, planet of disruption and change. You drift on the shifting currents of your feelings, never knowing quite where this or that sentiment could lead. One could carry you into a dark and fathomless trench, while another could set you comfortably into a dazzling sunny lagoon. For you, feelings are supremely real and supremely unpredictable.

For the Crab, feelings are also supremely real; however, since Cancer is ruled by the relatively predictable Moon, the tides of Cancerian emotions are often more steady than yours. Your new friend, in other words, can serve as a kind of safe harbor, providing you with the anchor that you need. This stability can manifest in many ways; one of the most likely has to do with money. Chances are that you don't really care much about finances; well, Crabs do. They like to know that their shell is safe, secured against the vagaries of fate and the myriad uncertainties of the deep. Once you realize that your favorite Crab wants you to share the tranquillity of its abode, your heart could just about melt.

Now, Crabs don't invite just anybody to share their shell. As noted earlier, they're timid souls, easily wounded and quick to retreat from the slings and arrows of life. Your remarkable sensitivity, however, has likely won the trust of your new friend, who realizes that there's no feeling, no matter how deep, that cannot be shared. Perhaps the only real danger threatening this match is the risk that, with your dreamy natures, you could kind of space out together on alcohol or drugs. (Not that you'd really do this, of course; we just need to account for all possibilities.) Avoid that pitfall, and the two of you could well be frolicking in the same sea for many years to come.

Pisces with Leo

JULY 24–AUGUST 23

Generally speaking, fire and water don't mix. And astrologically speaking, it should be clearly stated up front, the Lion and the Fish aren't among the zodiac's more compatible pairings. If you're considering a romance with a big cat, think twice: Felines, big and small, love to eat fish. No need to be overly dramatic; it's not impossible for this relationship to succeed. For it to truly prosper, however, you'll probably both have to work very hard. Is this love worth such toil? Only you, of course, can answer that question, but you might as well know ahead of time what you're in for.

From various points of view, it's hard to imagine a more diverse duo than a Lion and a Fish. Leo is one of the most outgoing creatures in the zodiac's great zoo; warm, temperamental, proud, regal, the king of beasts is the quintessential social animal. Leo is ruled by the Sun, source of life, and Lions consider themselves the life of the party, no matter where or what the party in question may be.

Okay, you say. So far, so good. After all, with your legendary adaptability, you can accommodate the big cat and its pride. Right? Well, you probably can, at least for a while. The question is, how will Leo accommodate you? Don't forget, Leo is a fixed sign; Lions are a bit set in their feelings and opinions. And though you're both very emotional, you live your feelings in different ways. Temperamental Leo is given—if not driven—to continual emotional outbursts; you tend to retreat into the world of your dreams. Leos don't like anyone to retreat. To them, it somehow seems unnatural. By now, you're probably beginning to get the picture. Lions can be rather self-absorbed, in a likable, extroverted kind of way. By their nature, Lions need plenty of feedback from just about everyone, and they have a tendency to insist that this feedback be flattering. Lions have a very high opinion of themselves and require everyone to join the chorus of praise.

If you do decide to proceed with this romance, you should know that the Lion will probably insist on dominating just about every aspect of your lives. Big cats like to rule. Now, this may not be all that bad. After all, you really don't care about such things as money, luxury, and so on, and Lions do. In fact, they love their creature comforts. The good life, they feel, is due them by birthright.

However, should the two of you take up housekeeping, you may find yourself paying dearly for it. Lions, you see, love to roam. You don't. The more your cat heads out on jungle jaunts, the more insecure you're likely to feel. And when you feel unloved, you can become a bit of a nag. This, in turn, could drive your new friend nuts. Something more for the two of you to work through.

And, though love always demands work, it should also be fulfilling and fun. Ultimately, you're probably both better off seeking that fulfillment elsewhere.

Pisces with Virgo

AUGUST 24–SEPTEMBER 23

When a Fish and a
Virgin get together, it's almost always an
illustration of the axiom "opposites at-
tract." Indeed, to find any considerable
affinities of heart or soul between the

two of you would be surprising. Not impossible, perhaps, but certainly surprising. So while this romance could serve as a pleasant casual fling, its long-term prospects are less promising. Sometimes, water plus earth can make arid land fertile; other times, all you get is mud.

For a while, of course, things could go along just fine, largely because each of you can offer qualities that the other lacks. Methodical, pragmatic, curious

Virgo, the mutable earth sign, could be quite attracted by your dreamy, romantic nature. "Here is someone so very different from me," your new friend might think. "I wonder just how this person works." Most Fish carry a fantastic world of imagination inside, and most Virgos don't. The rich world under the sea can seem intriguing, and your Virgo may want to dive in for a swim. You, meanwhile, could be attracted by your new friend's emotional warmth, humanitarian spirit, lively wit, and unmistakable charm. And with your lack of practical control over life's more mundane matters, from finances to laundry, you might enjoy having some willing support keeping things in order. Rest assured that the checkbook will always be balanced, the gas bill paid on time, the shopping list carefully drawn, and so on.

Convenient, yes? But not exactly

thrilling, at least not for a mystical romantic such as yourself. There are some other potential pitfalls as well. Virgo is a very mental sign, in a down-to-earth kind of way. Its natives relate to the world through a process of careful categorical thinking. They analyze (often), they deliberate (usually), they worry (endlessly), they try to accord each experience its proper place in the grand scheme of things, sometimes before they've even really lived it. And one other thing: Virgos love to find fault. Picture the two of you gazing at a blazing sunset; just as you're about to melt into the cosmic beauty of it all, your Virgo friend pipes up, "The view would really be so much nicer from that cliff. Too bad we're here, not there. Oh, well, some things just never work out." Sooner or later, this relentless criticism of just about everything in life is likely to get on your nerves. "Forget about trying to figure it all out!" you'll want to scream. "Who said life should fit your pictures? Just let yourself feel the moment!"

That, of course, is the problem. And chances are that your life in the bedroom won't rescue this relationship; not surprisingly, Virgins tend to be rather undemonstrative here, too. When they're discontented, they can turn downright prudish, which, for a romantic Piscean soul, can be the ultimate turnoff. Rather than save this romance, therefore, your sex life could mirror its shortcomings. It's not your friend's fault, of course, nor is it yours. You're both just being true to your astrological natures. Better for both of you to accept this wisely and end the relationship.

Pisces with Libra

SEPTEMBER 24–OCTOBER 23

Frankly, it's difficult to say just how a romance between these two signs will turn out. But that shouldn't prevent you from striking up a liaison with a Libran native, should the spirit move you. After all, in matters of the heart, there are no ultimate guarantees. And whatever the final destination of this relationship, the two of you will likely have a lot of fun along the way.

Libra, the cardinal air sign, is ruled by the planet Venus, named for the ancient god of beauty. Not surprisingly, those born under the sign of the Scales tend to have classic, well-balanced features; they also often flash a killer smile.

That Venusian smile has lit up many a heart; should it alight on you, you might find your heart instantly aglow. The glow could grow as you discover that there's much more to your new friend than just a pretty face. Libras can be quite romantic, charming, and elegant—this, you begin to think, could be the start of something big. Your Libra friend, meanwhile, might easily be lured by your depths of feeling, kindness, and mystical bent. Soon you both realize that many different levels of the self are in play, and before you know it, this affair has blossomed into a full-fledged relationship.

As your relationship progresses, the two of you will likely discover that you have plenty in common. And you might happen upon such discoveries in a delightfully random way—finding out, almost by coincidence, that you admire the same painters and writers, prefer the same wine, delight in the same little country inn. Indeed, the first months of your courtship could consist largely of a succession of strangely perfect outings— the museum one weekend, a night at the opera the next, and a romantic idyll in the country the next. You'll probably find that you both appreciate the finer things in life—the best hotels, gourmet cuisine, a spacious and comfortable home, and long sessions of tender lovemaking. And your heart could melt on discovering that, in spite of their elegant and self-possessed manner, the Scales are just as afraid of solitude as you are.

Don't be surprised, however, if, after a while, a few clouds appear on the horizon. This could have something to do with the subject of commitment. Although your Libran friend is indeed terrified of being alone, the Scales may be equally scared of the responsibility that comes with a truly serious relationship. Libra natives often have a narcissistic streak. As you'd expect of someone born under the sign of the Scales, when it comes time to make a major decision, they'll often endlessly weigh the options, consider the pros and cons, and then decide that they need to think about things a bit longer. The truth is, most Libras don't like to be tied down.

Such back-and-forth can tug plenty

on a person's heartstrings—particularly when someone is as sensitive and emotionally vulnerable as you. In the long run, you might get tired of waiting. If you do decide to part, however, you'll probably part friends, with each of you somehow more truly yourself for having known the other.

Pisces with Scorpio

OCTOBER 24–NOVEMBER 22

W*hen these two water*

signs get together, the result can be a love as vast, deep, and unpredictable as the great sea itself. Here, at last, is a sign with profundities of feeling comparable to yours. Both the Fish and the Scorpion are subject to emotional tides and undertows. And while you may navigate Neptune's domain in slightly different ways and will probably hit some tricky currents as well, your elemental natures are likely so powerfully in accord that many problems can be washed away. Even your shortcomings complement one another. You could instantly sense that you've met your soul mate. And chances are that your new friend will take one (or two) looks at you and say, "This Fish is a keeper."

You will come to the same conclusion surprisingly fast, since Scorpios are among the most impenetrable of all the zodiac's animals. How, then, can you get to know your new friend so quickly? The answer lies in the mysterious realm of the unspoken. The two of you may well share some ancient, mute knowledge, some sense that you've met before, either in this life or in another. This knowledge is communicated in many ways, but usually not through words. Foremost, perhaps, is the singular language of the body; there could be an instinctive attraction here, one that seems to awaken distant memories that approach and pass with a stately elegance, like a great ocean liner in the night. After the two of you meet, it could be weeks before you have a long and serious discussion; you'll be too busy getting acquainted to discuss the meaning of life.

As your relationship continues to deepen, you'll likely find that your new friend's stable core—Scorpio is, after all, a fixed sign—provides you with some welcome stability. For though mutable Fish are eternally adrift on the currents of feeling, Scorpios, with their biological links to terra firma, tend to be more solid. You both enjoy the staples of dating—restaurants, movies, concerts—yet your real encounters usually occur in the much more ethereal realms of the psyche and spirit. One exception: Not surprisingly, you likely both love romantic walks on the beach, gazing out over the ocean, and letting your dreams run wild. The ocean, of course, is a romantic place, and it's also your native abode. And it represents the collective unconscious, among whose archetypes you're both now making your astonished way.

Of course, any relationship this profound, particularly between these two water signs, will stir up a few haunting denizens of the deep. Scorpio is ruled by the planet Pluto, named for the ancient god of the underworld; in astrology, Pluto also represents the pull of the past—dormant wounds that might reawaken as the two of you get closer.

Should this occur, there may well be a few stormy seas, and it's worth remembering that the Scorpion's tail can really sting. Fortunately, however, your sensitivity should help disarm otherwise dangerous disagreements. And Scorpio's legendary possessiveness, which would scare away many other signs, doesn't bother you in the slightest; it's just further proof that you're truly loved. It's hard to imagine, for the two of you, a more perfect union.

Pisces with Sagittarius

NOVEMBER 23–DECEMBER 21

A *romance between a* Fish and an Archer should test you both. As the mutable water sign, of course, you're ruled by Neptune, named for the ancient god of the sea. Before Sag's current planetary ruler, Jupiter, was discovered, Neptune also ruled Sagittarius. What does this mean in terms of love? Well, there are several intriguing possibilities. It stands to reason (astrologically speaking, that is) that you'll fascinate each other. Will this fascination prove compelling and enduring enough to outweigh your many differences? This is, like life itself, an open question.

From the beginning of your relationship, you'll find yourselves linked by a spiritual bond; however, you may discover that you approach the life of the spirit in slightly different ways. Fish operate on an instinctive level; swimming around in the great sea of the human unconscious, you're often able to pass quickly beyond the rational level of life and see directly into the myriad mysteries of the depths. This capacity can particularly fascinate the Archer, whose bow is usually aimed in the other direction toward the no less abundant wonders of the spirit. The Archer's transcendent yearning, in turn, awakens the latent nostalgia of your soul; the two of you just may wind up meeting in that magical realm where the heights of the spirit and the depths of the psyche meet.

Should that indeed occur, you may find yourselves facing the first great test of your love. Romantic Fish such as yourself yearn with all your being to find the soul mate who can unlock the final mystery of your nature. For you, this love could quickly become everything, and you'll be ready to settle down. If so, you'll need to be careful just how you present all of this to your Sag friend, since in matters of the heart, as in everything else, Archers love to roam. Even if your friend is utterly smitten, he could need plenty of time before he feels comfortable closing the gate to the corral. You'll have to find a way to grant your Archer the necessary freedom, and your new friend will need to provide you with the reassurance you crave.

The French have a saying reminding us that "one oncoming train sometimes hides another." Well, if your love weathers its first test, there could be another trial fast on its heels. With your remarkable Piscean sensitivity to other people's emotions, you could be a bit shocked by your Sagittarian friend's habit of blurting out painful truths. Indeed, you could find your Archer astonishingly insensitive; your friend, in turn, could find you almost unbearably touchy. Perhaps it will help to realize that neither of you is actually trying to hurt the other; you are, after all, just being true to your natures.

Happily, you'll be able to smooth

over such little differences in the bed-room, where your spiritual affinities are marvelously translated into the domain of the flesh. So even though this may not be an easy romance, it'll certainly be a challenging one, sure to allow you both to grow in many wonderful ways—and, who knows, it'll maybe grant you the magic of a lifelong love as well.

Pisces with Capricorn

DECEMBER 22–JANUARY 20

In *affairs of the heart,*
the Fish and the Goat are a curious combination. It's not that the two of you have all that much in common, really, al-

though you certainly do share certain values and opinions that can allow your love to unfold naturally of its own accord. What makes this match surprisingly promising is the way your rather diverse natures complement each other. As a water sign, you can make Capricorn's immense inner terrain fertile, while the Goat's down-to-earth influence can give you the structure you need to grow. Sounds quite magical, but in astrological terms such matters are really elementary.

As the mutable water sign, you Fish often manifest a particular tendency toward emotional insecurity. It's nothing serious: Since you tend to be extremely sensitive, both to your emotions and to those of the people around you, it's easy to get pulled along on various currents of feeling and wind up occasionally losing touch with your own center. You might well, therefore, be drawn to your Goat's deeply rooted stability and remarkable tranquillity of heart and soul. While, for you, life is a vast sea of feeling, to Goats, life appears as a mountain to be carefully climbed. You Fish can never be certain where the next current will carry you; Goats carefully plan their ascent in order to be sure to reach the summit. Such certainty could stand you in good stead; even the most dreamy of Pisceans can use a little advance planning.

On the other hand, with typical Capricorn reserve, your new friend could perhaps use a little help getting in touch with feelings. You should be warned: For many Goats this is very hard to do! These animals need to feel safe with someone before they can begin to relax that cool and aloof appearance and admit that, however independent they may be, they also want to be loved. With your remark-able emotional sensitivity, you can recognize—and accept—exactly where your new friend is coming from, without the Goat even saying a word. As this Capricorn begins to sense the quiet depths behind your soothing manner, it can relax, open up, and finally share those deepest hopes and fears. The understanding and trust that has thus so easily grown between you can provide your love with a strong and sure foundation.

Other factors also bode well for this

pair. With your easy adaptability, you may help soften your new friend's admittedly rigid opinions, while you could find your pronounced proclivity for sentimental indulgence nicely offset by your Goat's rather more arid cast of mind. Your penchant for straying into deep and murky waters has led some to say that Pisces is the sign of its own undoing; in this regard, the Goat could save you from the darker side of yourself. You can return the favor in the bedroom, where your tender patience can allow this earth sign to release the volcano that lies within.

Pisces with Aquarius

JANUARY 21–FEBRUARY 19

There's no question that Fish and Water Bearers have a lot in common. Chances are, however, that your differences will surpass your affinities.

Most important, as air signs, Aquarians look at life through the mind, while you Fish regard experience through your feelings. So if you're considering falling in love with a high-flying Aquarian, you should realize going in that some compromises will likely be necessary in order for this relationship to work.

At first glance, however, there are plenty of reasons why the two of you might, for a while at least, become an item. With your gentle and kind nature, you could easily be moved by your Aquarian friend's altruistic concern for humanity. And the Water Bearer's general openness to communication could lead you to believe that you've found someone capable of truly sharing your heart. Aquarians, with their love of spiritual adventure, could easily be lured by your mystical streak and find themselves tempted to sound the ample depths of a

Pisces soul. You'll likely discover that you have many interests in common. You're both creative by nature and could easily enjoy each other's company, making the rounds at art galleries, museums, and concert halls—not to mention the occasional romantic dinner in a gourmet restaurant.

It almost goes without saying that, as a water sign, you're likely more in touch with your feelings than most Aquarians

are with theirs. Don't be surprised, however, if you're more in touch with your
lover's feelings as well. After all, as the
fixed air sign, Aquarian natives are usually
much more at home in the lofty realms of
thought than in the murky depths of
emotions. For them, love is an ideal; while
they find it easy to love humanity in general, loving one person in particular can
prove more difficult.

As a result of such differences, your

relationship could, in spite of its many strengths, find itself sailing into some rather rough waters. When you get to the bottom of these troubled seas, you just may find that, although Water Bearers consider feelings a part of life, by no means do they consider them everything. For Fish, however, emotions are the very stuff of creation, and you're always in a state of flux. For this relationship to long endure, you're both going to have to find a new way to relate to your feelings. Since you're so deeply in touch with the emotional side of your nature, you can be sensitive to the slightest alterations—real or apparent—in the dynamic between the two of you. In spite of their name, Water Bearers are likely to find such constant (they would say relentless) emotionality, well, difficult to bear.

As your relationship proceeds, then, you may both begin to feel that neither of you is really in your element. After all, Fish don't fly, and Water Bearers keep their feelings in a jug or an urn, where they can be safely dispensed in manageable doses. Aquarians are among the most independent of souls, and after a while this one may increasingly long for the limpid heights of the clear azure. If so, let it go; there are plenty of Fish in the sea.

Pisces with Pisces

FEBRUARY 20–MARCH 20

Should you fall in love with another Fish, you'll likely find a relationship rich with potential and fraught with potential problems. You can be sure, however, that no matter how things turn out, this is one romance that will definitely never be boring.

There's no mystery why two Fish would hit it off. First, you both spend your lives in the same ocean, so there's a strong likelihood that, sooner or later, you'll swim across each other's path. And when you do, whether you meet in a warm, sunny turquoise lagoon or the chilly, murky depths of the Atlantic, you may both feel that you've found that long-lost other half of yourself. Many of you Fish don't feel really whole and complete unless you're loved by a special someone; you eternally navigate the tricky currents of river and stream, lake and ocean, in search of the perfect passion that'll bring fulfillment and ultimate meaning to your life. Now, you both think, maybe, just maybe, your respective dreams are coming true at last.

And, quite possibly, they are. You have virtually everything in common, from an interest in mysticism to a fondness for seafood, champagne, diamonds, and fairy tales with happy endings. The idyllic early days of your relationship could be spent watching the sun set into the ocean on late afternoon strolls, hiking in the mountains, and cooking up meals together at home. In the bedroom, meanwhile, you're both adventurous;

your lovemaking is just that—an expression of the rich and complex world of feelings that the two of you share. It's also, incidentally, probably a lot of fun.

The only problem with all this is that, however much you may both hate to admit it, there's more to life than walks on the beach and rolls in the hay. For many of you Fish, love is a way of completing what's missing in your own personality. And, to be perfectly frank, the problem here is that the two of you may be missing some of the same ingredients. When it comes to practical matters, chances are that you're both equally help-less—in this relationship, who is going to balance the checkbook? More serious, however, is the possibility that you both have a tendency to wallow in self-pity; as long as you have a suitable partner, this aspect of your personality can be kept in the background, where it belongs. The two of you together, however, could just spend your days and nights whining, crying, and feeling sorry for yourselves. Finally, you both can easily become very dependent; this relationship, therefore, could become dangerously inverted, turned in upon itself.

All this is just a bit too harsh, of course, exaggerated for the sake of effect, and warning you of the one potential pitfall that could mar an otherwise splendid romance. As long as you both check in from time to time with the real world, you might find that this is indeed the romance you've dreamed of for so long. And this is where we'll leave you—frolicking happily in the great ocean of your love, having found that special person with whom you get along, well, swimmingly.

You and the Moon

Just as the Moon takes a month to orbit the Earth, so it requires approximately thirty days to pass through, or transit, the various signs of the zodiac—beginning with Aries, ending with Pisces, and spending about two and a half days in each. As it does so, it exerts an extraordinary influence on our moods, much as it expends a mysterious, physical pull on the ocean's tides.

The Sun may guide our more conscious and overt qualities, but the Moon rules over our instinctive, intuitive life; when we examine our daily moon signs, we become aware of the myriad and mystical ways in which that lunar body affects our emotional weather. When it transits a fire sign, for example, we are often dominated by fiery emotions, such as anger and passion. As it moves to an earth sign, we will feel a more rooted need for stability and comfort. The Moon in a water sign will generally bring watery emotions, like sadness and confusion; and an air-sign passage will lead to a sharpening of our thirst for knowledge.

Obviously, emotional weather isn't identical for everyone; the relationship between the position of the Moon and your particular sun sign will influence what the precise mood of the moment will be for you, and a constant subtle interplay occurs. If we pay close attention to the passages of the Moon, however, we can become far more adept at negotiating wisely and well the many challenges and changes of our daily life.

(Consult the moon charts beginning on page 332 for the time and date that the Moon enters each of the twelve signs of the zodiac throughout every month of the year from 1997 to 2005.)

The Moon in Aries

When the Moon moves into the sign of the Ram, energies run high and people tend to get aggressive, assertive, and even a bit irritated. Since Aries is of the fire element, passions have a way of burning out of control, which can prove particularly trying for Fish, whose emotions always simmer near the surface. With your sensitivities to other people's moods, you'll want to be sure not to take on their negativity over the next couple of days. Steer clear of potential problems—there's no need to tempt the lunar gods.

In any case, you'll likely find yourself brimming with energy, which, given your rather sleepy nature, isn't always the case. When you're in the mood, it's fine to be active, but when you're not . . . well, nothing and nobody can force you. Don't be surprised, however, if you suddenly find yourself hankering for action. And if you do feel that way, open up to the flow and take advantage of the many benefits that an Aries Moon can confer.

Just what should you do with all your vim and vigor? Well, the fact that

Aries is a cardinal sign makes this a perfect time to get involved with new activities and to create something. It's possible that at work, for example, you might want to go ahead and launch that new project you've been dreaming about for so long; the Aries Moon favors selling, marketing, and advertising.

However, for artistically minded Fish, the chances are greater that you've got some personal project percolating on the back burner; if so, this is the time to move it up to the front of the stove. Maybe you've been mulling over a painting or sculpture for the last few months; well, get out your paints or your clay and start translating your vision into reality.

For most humans, however, the energy of the Aries Moon is too hot for any sedentary activities. You might want to burn off some of that heat by heading for the nearest tennis courts or stopping off at the gym for a brisk workout. Come evening, don't waste time on the movies or theater; head for the hottest disco in town, where you can dance the night away. And don't be surprised if your sexuality suddenly ignites—the Aries Moon can turn the warm glow of Piscean feeling into a scorching flame.

263

The Moon in Taurus

The *transiting Moon* passing into the sign of the Bull offers you an opportunity to get grounded. Fish like you tend to inhabit two worlds—the mystical world of spirit and feeling as well as the "real" world. Indeed, for you, the "real" world often seems much less interesting than the fascinating universe of dreams you harbor deep within. Taurus, of the fixed quality and the earth element, is the most practical sign of the zodiac. In other words, let the down-to-earth vibes of the Taurus Moon help you take care of business.

To begin with, balance your checkbook, then plan your budget for the next month or so. While you doubtless find few activities in life less appealing, they have to be done sometime, so you might as well catch a ride on some favorable lunar vibes. At work, this isn't a propitious moment to boldly launch new projects. Hunker down, play your cards close to the vest, and steer clear of any colleagues with whom you might be on less than ideal terms. And should there be a big deal waiting to be completed, consider putting off final negotiations for a few days, until the Moon passes into the sign of the Twins.

Similarly, in your personal life the Taurus Moon bodes ill for communication. Fish like you, of course, often have something urgent to say about how you feel. However, if you've been waiting to have a big heart-to-heart with that special someone, you're probably wise to wait a day or two in order to profit from the Gemini Moon's beneficent glow. Some Pisceans will find this to be a real challenge, but in the long run you may both benefit. For now, it's better to let sleeping Bulls lie.

Fortunately, there are plenty of other activities with which you can occupy yourself. Since this is a mellow time, you may not exactly feel like working out for three hours; if not, don't force it. Kick back, relax, work in your garden, lounge under the big elm tree in your backyard. No elm tree? Well, browse the local antique stores; there's no telling what bargains you might find. Come evening, enjoy a good dinner and a fine wine; then head for the bedroom, which the soft rays of the Taurus Moon can transform into a garden of earthly delights.

The Moon in Gemini

When the Moon passes from slow Taurus into the sign of the quick-witted Twins, look for your life to light up in a big way. Ruled by the planet Mercury, named for the ancient messenger of the gods, Gemini favors communication, laughter, and general good times.

Of course, unless these two and a half days fall on a weekend, you'll still have to go to work. In this arena, the Twins highlight advertising, marketing, and effective discussion—this is a good time for staff meetings, planning sessions, and general strategy. And if you're on the verge of finalizing a big contract, you can use these lunar vibes to help you negotiate the last details.

When it comes to communication in your personal life, the Gemini influence can also prove particularly favorable. Odds are that Fish like you love to talk about your emotions. The problem is, sometimes you can get a bit lost, drifting around on all those deep currents of feeling. Perhaps in your romantic relationship you've got a big conversation looming ahead. Well, since the Gemini

Moon emphasizes intellect over sentiment, its vibes could actually help you clarify those murky emotional waters and infuse your discussion with a little welcome lightness. And if you've gleaned a few new insights about yourself, go ahead and jot them down in your journal; the Gemini Moon bodes well for the written word.

It wouldn't be surprising, therefore, if you suddenly feel like relaxing at home with a good book. Or should this Moon fall on a weekend, you may be seized by a yearning to get away for a day or two. If so, go with it; a weekend in the country could be just what the stars have ordered.

Should you decide to hang around home, however, you'll likely find plenty of fun as well. If you've been invited to a big society bash but, with your Piscean self-doubt, are wondering whether you'll fit in, go ahead and take the chance—you might just have a blast. Or if there's nothing that exciting on your social calendar, create a little excitement of your own. Invite some friends over for an impromptu party; chances are that everyone will hit it off delightfully, and they'll have you to thank. However powerful the deep currents of romance may be, it's always worth remembering how much a few good friends can really mean.

The Moon in Cancer

When the Moon passes into the moody sign of the Crab, feelings often come to the fore, particularly for Fish. Indeed, under the influence of this cardinal water sign, the Moon highlights those emotional aspects of your life that you feel most ardently anyway; as a result, the next two and a half days could be rather intense.

It's a good idea to retreat just a bit, like the Crab going back in his shell, and safely take stock of the many currents of feeling swirling around. Of course, you'll probably wish to follow some; others may threaten to lead you into deeper and darker waters than you care to probe, at least at this point. As an experienced navigator of the ocean of feelings, you know that certain denizens of the unlit depths may, for all their opaque potencies, prove rather frightful. Better, perhaps, to content yourself for the moment with a pleasantly temperate, sun-infused blue lagoon.

During these few days, don't be surprised to find yourself longing for the warmth and security of home and family.

You might be best off puttering around the house—replacing a broken washer, cleaning out the garage, putting up a new bookcase, and so on. If you do go out, why not stop by the antique store, just in case that special vase has miraculously come in (the Moon's vibes, after all, have worked bigger wonders)? Or perhaps you find yourself overwhelmed by a passionate yearning to do absolutely nothing at all. If so, read, meditate, or take a nap.

Feel free to follow this prompting of your heart and soul; they might just be trying to let you know that it's time to slow down a bit, allowing everything to quiet down so you can hear—and heed—what's really going on inside. Don't feel guilty about relaxing, because you'll practically be a social butterfly when the Moon is in Leo.

Now that you've enjoyed an afternoon of true repose, how about cooking up a special dinner for your family or several good friends, just to let everyone know how much they mean to you? Of course, you could also opt to dine out with a single special someone—in a romantic restaurant for a leisurely feast lit by candles. After all, some tides of feeling are best followed *á deux*.

The Moon in Leo

After the intensity of the last few days, you may be a bit relieved to encounter the outgoing and upbeat mood that generally accompanies a Leo Moon. You Pisces natives can tend to get a bit wrapped up in the complexities of your own—and other people's—feelings; the next few days can offer you a welcome opportunity to forget about your cares and simply let the good times roll.

When the Moon is in the sign of the good-natured Lion, social relationships of all sorts tend to benefit from the warm lunar vibes. This is the perfect time to be with people. At the office, you

might want to pay close attention to net-
working; the connections you cultivate
now could come in handy sooner than
you think. Don't make a big project of it,
however; do what you feel comfortable
doing—there's no point in forcing
things. And remember: Under a Leo
Moon, people's egos can become just a
bit touchy. (The Lion is, after all, the
king of the jungle.) As long as you exercise your natural sensitivity, you should

do just fine. This is not, by the way, a particularly good time to pursue more formal matters: If there are legal affairs to be negotiated, for example, you're much better off waiting a few days for the Moon to leave Leo, transit through Virgo, and enter the sign of the Scales.

When it comes to your personal life, you may as well allow yourself to relax, kick back, and enjoy. Have you been invited to a couple of parties this weekend and are wondering which to attend? Well, why not hit them all? You might just (presuming, of course, that you're in the market) encounter a romantic surprise. In any case, all these gatherings will likely boast a particularly festive air, with plenty of good, clean fun.

Otherwise, get together with family and a few good friends for an evening out at the movies or, better yet, at the opera or theater; Leo, after all, loves performances. If you're romantically unattached, you may want to go ahead and attend a singles event, even if you normally avoid such affairs—this one just might be different. And if you do have a special someone, you may prefer to limit your socializing to the two of you; Leo's fire plus Pisces' water can make for a very steamy scene.

The Moon in Virgo

Now *that you've re-*laxed and enjoyed yourself a bit, you may find that you're hankering to get back to less frivolous matters as the Moon passes into the sign of the Virgin. The lunar influence of the mutable earth sign, in fact, makes this an ideal time for your normally dreamy soul to emerge from the watery depths of feeling and, for a few days at least, look after life on good old terra firma.

Chances are that during the Crab and Leo Moons, you forgot all about those boring and, shall we say, down-to-earth concerns that from time to time must occupy your mind. How long has it been, for example, since you really went through that stack of unpaid bills? Well, as you may have had occasion to discover, when it comes to bills, what you don't pay can hurt you. In other words, sit down, get out your checkbook, a pen, and a roll of stamps, and take care of business. And while you're at it, check your budget for the rest of the month as well. All this may be less painful than you think; the Virgo Moon shines kindly on

just such pragmatic, detail-oriented tasks.
Once that's done, you might discover
that there's enough in the bank to allow
you to spend a leisurely afternoon perus-
ing the local flea markets, perhaps pick-
ing up a little knickknack to brighten
your home.

Generally (there are, of course, occasional exceptions), the Virgo Moon
bodes ill for most kinds of social gatherings. People somehow just don't seem to

be in the mood for relaxing and having fun; at times, folks can get downright ornery. And, not surprisingly, the Virgin Moon rarely bodes well for the physical side of romance, so don't be surprised if neither you nor your partner is hot to trot. If you do give it a try and things don't work out as well as usual, don't worry; when the Moon enters Libra in a day or two, everything should be just fine.

In the meantime, look after your diet—are you eating as well as you should? Make a few plans for the future. Settle down with a good book. Spend a few hours jotting down your thoughts in your journal. Focus quietly on your own inner life; soon enough, the outward life will follow.

The Moon in Libra

Ruled by the planet Venus, named for the ancient goddess of love and beauty, Libra is one of the most romantic signs in the entire zodiac. So when the silvery luminary passes into the sign of the Scales, look for your love life to warm up in a hurry.

Even during the Libra Moon, however, most people have to work, and you'll be happy to know that the good lunar vibes of the next few days can augur professional as well as personal affairs. You'll likely sense a cooperative spirit in the air, which you can turn to your advantage should you have any outstanding contracts or deals that need a bit of final negotiation.

With such concerns now out of the way, you're free to follow the promptings of your heart. These few days are likely a good time for just about everything, with the possible exception of physical exercise. Most people, particularly Pisceans such as yourself, feel a bit disinclined to tire themselves out at the gym, perhaps because you feel that there are, uh, more important Fish to fry.

Perhaps you've held your tongue over the last few days, waiting for a favorable Moon to have that heart-to-heart talk with someone special. Well, wait no longer: Even the most thorny topics could melt under the Libra Moon's gentle glow. This is also a time to appreciate beauty in all its forms, from masterpieces of art (perhaps an afternoon at a museum is in order) to masterpieces of nature. And don't forget your own beauty as well; stop off at a nearby spa for a little pampering of body and soul.

Now you're really ready to party. If you feel in the mood, call up a few friends and suggest an impromptu gathering, full of good food and hearty camaraderie. As the night wears on, why not head for the hottest nightclub in town to take in a few tunes and dance till you're ready to drop? And, by the way, if you're currently unattached, this outing just might wind up with a surprising romantic encounter.

If you're in a relationship, of course, you may prefer to limit the evening to just the two of you. Reserve a quiet table at your favorite restaurant, where you can whisper sweet nothings to your hearts' content; then head home to enjoy the Libra Moon's gentle caress well into the night.

The Moon in Scorpio

As *the transiting Moon* departs gentle Libra and enters the darker realm of the Scorpion, you should prepare yourself for a brief sojourn in a zone of intense emotional turbulence.

This doesn't always happen, of course, and there's no certainty that a storm will break. But there will undoubtedly be a few clouds on the horizon. Don't forget that Scorpio is ruled by the planet Pluto, named for the ancient god of the underworld and the dead. In astrology, Pluto has long been seen as a somber and disturbing influence, associated with the darkly destructive forces of the psyche, making the Scorpio Moon fraught with many potential problems.

Often, this tendency is demonstrated by people who suddenly feel the need to dredge up all sorts of old wounds, both real and imagined, convinced that the bright rays of day will, so to speak, dissipate the bitter clouds that seem to appear from time to time. Of course, Fish like yourself, experienced in the nuances of emotional life, know well enough how dark clouds can also carry hot lightning. Moral of this metaphor: Don't go out in the storm unless you have to. In other words, over the next few days you may want to retreat a bit, take shelter in the warm waters of your inner self, and allow the storm above to blow itself out. When you're safely settled in the depths, the surface waves, however furiously they might crash and swell, are quite harmless indeed.

Okay, you say. But what exactly

should you do? Or not do? Well, to begin with, you're better off avoiding discussions with family, friends, lovers, colleagues, and just about anyone else. If you can't avoid them, keep your encounters simple and superficial. No need to stir anything up. Similarly, the Pluto Moon bodes ill for most forms of social life. If you throw a party, your guests could wind up hurling food at one another. A simple family dinner could wind up looking like a modern-dress version of *Oedipus Rex*. (Maybe not quite *that* bad.)

However, you're still better off turning inward and focusing on yourself. Enjoy the tranquil silence of your inner depths. Thus refreshed, you might find yourself hankering for the bedroom—good sex is one of the best ways to transform Scorpio's dark desires into regenerative joy and tenderness.

The Moon in Sagittarius

Now *that you have*
weathered the Scorpion's storms, you've
earned the right to enjoy the many bless-
ings brought by the Sagittarius Moon.
Over the next few days, people's thoughts

tend to turn to the big topics, as if people somehow vaguely suspect that the humdrum events of daily life aren't quite exalted enough to justify their brief sojourn on this planet. You dreamy Pisceans, of course, are rarely lost in the mundane, for the simple reason that you avoid it like the plague. Well, over the next few days you might discover that even the most down-to-earth person has, at least for the moment, an altruistic interest in the greater things.

As you know well enough, Fish such as yourself generally approach life more through your feelings than through your intellect, so you're likely to be particularly influenced by the Sag Moon's emphasis on lively and upbeat emotions, which it blends with liberal doses of open-mindedness. This is, in other words, a time to open up to the mysteries of life, to follow your inclination for learning wherever it might lead. Perhaps, for example, you've thought about enrolling in an evening class in order to learn about a new software program, or you've been wanting to explore such topics as spiritual healing. No matter. Whatever path opens before you, step into it boldly. This can also be true, by the way, of certain activities at work, where it's a good time for holding staff meetings, finalizing sales, and taking care of legal matters.

If there's one activity most favored by the Sagittarius Moon, it probably is travel. The Archer, you see, loves to roam. So, should this be a weekend or holiday, how about getting away from it all, to the mountains, the country, or the sea? The sudden change in scenery could work wonders. And, in a similar vein, if you've been thinking about booking a major vacation—to Europe or the Caribbean, for example—why not take advantage of some favorable lunar vibrations and set your plan into action?

Of course, you'll find plenty of fun available closer to home as well. Work off your overflowing energy with a trip to the gym. Or get in a few sets of tennis. Or stay right at home—after all, there's no better place than the bedroom to bask in the Sagittarian Moon's beneficent glow.

The Moon in Capricorn

When the Moon passes into the sign of the Goat, don't be surprised if the more down-to-earth and serious side of life seems to take center stage. This is the Moon under which you will have one of your rare bursts of domesticity; you'll fly around the house dusting, vacuuming, and scrubbing the kitchen floor until it shines. Usually, if given the chance, you can while away hours at a time just daydreaming. Not under this Moon!

Capricorn is one of the most ambitious signs in the zodiac; the Goat is known for carefully planning its way up the mountain of life. For you Fish, of course, life is more a turbulent ocean to be navigated through the powers of intuition than a mountain to be carefully and strategically scaled. However, as a wise man once said, "If you don't know where you want to go, you shouldn't be surprised if you never get there."

This is, alas, at least somewhat true for everyone, even for you. So you might as well use the next few days to begin making some long-range plans—to take a clear and sober look at where you've been, where you are today, and where you want to go in the future. Many Fish have a tendency to look at life (their own life included) through rose-colored glasses; in other words, it's easy for you to lose touch with what is actually going on, to mistake your dreams for reality. You might want to use the Goat's lunar vibes to see if you can penetrate the veil of sentiment that may surround you and allow reality to emerge undiluted by fantasy and desire. It may appear a bit harsh, at first; however, there's personal power to be gained from bathing in the truth.

Once you do this, you'll have an important advantage over many other signs. You know already that fate reserves plenty of surprises as you make your way along the forked path of life: Whatever plan you devise is at best a rough blueprint, not an infallible guide. The future, particularly for Fish such as yourself, is always subject to the shifting currents of feeling and fate. Yet it can't hurt to have at least a rough topography of the ocean floor to help you along the way.

Once you've taken stock of things, you may want to look after a few practical tasks. At work, handle negotiations and other pragmatic details, which will come easily to you under the Capricorn Moon. Otherwise, pick up some new

clothing and a few needed items for the
house; if you have children, this would be
a good time to organize a crafts day for
yourself and the kids or otherwise relax
in the casual comfort of hearth and
home.

The Moon in Aquarius

Should you find your-self undergoing a major mood swing, don't be surprised: The Moon's passage from practical Capricorn to visionary Aquarius can result in one of the month's most striking transformations of lunar energy, particularly for such dreamers as you. After all the sober reflection of the last few days, you may suddenly find your spirit airborne.

As the fixed air sign, Aquarius is often one of the most radical phases of the Moon. As with the Capricorn Moon, the emphasis is on the future—however, not as something to be carefully planned for but as something to be created in the crucible of vision. And for all of the Water Bearer's legendary independence, this vision is created communally through the free exchange of ideas. While Aquarian energy often tends toward the trendy, it can also awaken deeper, less faddish modes of thinking. Of course, you Pisceans have in the depths of your soul a mystical streak that corresponds perfectly with this part of the Aquarian vision; as a result, don't hesitate to say what you think about matters of the spirit; you just may find that during the next few days your ideas will be widely welcomed.

Plunge wholeheartedly into creative endeavors, such as writing, composing, and painting. Even if you don't normally consider yourself an artist, you might discover that you have something important to say. If so, out with it! Otherwise, the Aquarian Moon bodes well for travel, for exploring the outer as well as the inner world. Where should you go? Avoid the seashore, unless you feel an overwhelming desire to bask in the sights and sounds of your native element. You're better off heading for the mountains, to a nearby resort, or just about anywhere else.

Under this Moon, romance often wanes, at least for a day or two, since Aquarius is a sign of the mind, not of the heart. No big deal, though. This is a good time for meeting with people, talking, and exchanging thoughts and ideas on all kinds of topics, from political issues of today to the future of humanity. So if you find your romantic ardor momentarily cooled, why not invite over some friends for casual conversation and a bite to eat? After all, they're living under the same lunar beams that you are, and there's no reason you can't all take advantage of the altruistic spirit of the Aquarian Moon.

The Moon in Pisces

The Moon's passage through your own sign is a time rich with potential, as well as possible pitfalls. Use the lunar energy well and the next few days can be immensely advantageous.

Use it poorly, however, and you might find yourself awash in a sea of troubles.

Foremost, you need to realize that the Pisces Moon tends to cloud people's judgment. This is true for all the creatures in the zodiac's great zoo, but it's particularly true for Fish. Chances are that you're by nature prone to occasional bouts of slightly fuzzy thinking; if you're not careful, the next few days could prove quite confusing. How should you deal with this? Well, remember that whatever you're thinking will probably change with the transiting Moon, so don't lend too much credence to passing fancies. Avoid making any irrevocable decisions, no matter how much you may feel like it. Do you suddenly seem sure that getting married to your partner is the best way to help your relationship progress? Well, maybe it is. But then again, maybe it's not. Wait a week or so for the Moon to exit the sign of the Fish, pass through Aries, and enter the pragmatic domain of the Bull. If you still want to get hitched, fine. If you don't, you'll be quite glad you waited.

You may want to focus your energies on creative endeavors, such as music, poetry, and art. Take in a concert or spend a leisurely afternoon strolling through a museum. You may also find that your usual sensitivity to the emotions of others is particularly acute. This is a time when people tend to wallow just a bit in self-pity. If friends seek your advice, go ahead and listen patiently; you do that so well, after all. When it comes time to dispense advice, however, remember that the Pisces Moon may be playing a few tricks with your judgment, too. Generally, over the next few days it's a good idea for everyone to give his feelings plenty of room to roam.

What should you do with all this emotion? Take a trip to the beach, go for a swim, or curl up with a good book. And don't be disappointed should your own love life seem a bit unclear; these currents of feeling have a way of stirring up some sediment. When the Moon enters fiery Aries, things should heat up just fine.

Moon

Charts

1997 – 2005

T

he preceding section, "You and the Moon,"

explained in detail how the Moon affects your emotions and behavior as it moves through the twelve signs of the zodiac. It takes approximately thirty days for the Moon to pass through, or transit, the twelve signs—spending about two and a half days in each. So every month, for the short period that the Moon is moving through Leo, or Aries, or Scorpio (or any other sign), you can take advantage of the Moon's positive or negative influences.

The following charts show the date
and time the Moon enters each sign of
the zodiac. Just look up the current date
(charts are provided for the years 1997
through 2005); the sign that precedes the
date indicates the Moon's current transit.
For instance, in the two following transits

Can Jan 10 19:43

Leo Jan 13 02:45

the Moon enters the sign of Cancer on

January 10 at 19:43 (7:43 P.M.) and stays in that sign until entering the sign of Leo on January 13 at 02:45 (2:45 A.M.). All times are eastern standard time in a twenty-four-hour clock format: 00:01–12:00 (noon) are the A.M. hours; 12:01–24:00 (midnight) are the P.M. hours (from 13:00 to 24:00, subtract 12 to translate into P.M.).

1997

	Sag Feb 01 23:49	Aqu Mar 05 14:53
Sco Jan 03 08:00	Cap Feb 04 03:43	Pis Mar 07 14:56
Sag Jan 05 14:26	Aqu Feb 06 04:20	Ari Mar 09 14:32
Cap Jan 07 16:54	Pis Feb 08 03:33	Tau Mar 11 15:38
Aqu Jan 09 16:59	Ari Feb 10 03:29	Gem Mar 13 19:49
Pis Jan 11 16:50	Tau Feb 12 05:56	Can Mar 16 03:51
Ari Jan 13 18:21	Gem Feb 14 11:54	Leo Mar 18 15:08
Tau Jan 15 22:40	Can Feb 16 21:12	Vir Mar 21 03:59
Gem Jan 18 05:53	Leo Feb 19 08:52	Lib Mar 23 16:34
Can Jan 20 15:28	Vir Feb 21 21:38	Sco Mar 26 03:41
Leo Jan 23 02:50	Lib Feb 24 10:22	Sag Mar 28 12:38
Vir Jan 25 15:26	Sco Feb 26 21:55	Cap Mar 30 19:06
Lib Jan 28 04:21	Sag Mar 01 07:00	Aqu Apr 01 22:57
Sco Jan 30 15:47	Cap Mar 03 12:37	Pis Apr 04 00:41

Ari Apr 06 01:19	Gem May 07 15:21	Leo Jun 08 14:58
Tau Apr 08 02:21	Can May 09 21:13	Vir Jun 11 02:43
Gem Apr 10 05:27	Leo May 12 06:32	Lib Jun 13 15:35
Can Apr 12 12:04	Vir May 14 18:43	Sco Jun 16 02:50
Leo Apr 14 22:22	Lib May 17 07:26	Sag Jun 18 10:37
Vir Apr 17 11:00	Sco May 19 18:11	Cap Jun 20 15:01
Lib Apr 19 23:35	Sag May 22 01:49	Aqu Jun 22 17:20
Sco Apr 22 10:17	Cap May 24 06:50	Pis Jun 24 19:08
Sag Apr 24 18:31	Aqu May 26 10:19	Ari Jun 26 21:38
Cap Apr 27 00:31	Pis May 28 13:17	Tau Jun 29 01:23
Aqu Apr 29 04:49	Ari May 30 16:17	Gem Jul 01 06:35
Pis May 01 07:49	Tau Jun 01 19:39	Can Jul 03 13:33
Ari May 03 09:59	Gem Jun 03 23:55	Leo Jul 05 22:45
Tau May 05 12:04	Can Jun 06 06:01	Vir Jul 08 10:22

Lib Jul 10 23:20	Sag Aug 12 04:44	Aqu Sep 12 23:08
Sco Jul 13 11:19	Cap Aug 14 10:40	Pis Sep 14 23:58
Sag Jul 15 20:01	Aqu Aug 16 12:57	Ari Sep 16 23:25
Cap Jul 18 00:44	Pis Aug 18 13:00	Tau Sep 18 23:22
Aqu Jul 20 02:28	Ari Aug 20 12:45	Gem Sep 21 01:39
Pis Jul 22 02:59	Tau Aug 22 13:58	Can Sep 23 07:33
Ari Jul 24 04:03	Gem Aug 24 17:56	Leo Sep 25 17:12
Tau Jul 26 06:53	Can Aug 27 01:11	Vir Sep 28 05:27
Gem Jul 28 12:04	Leo Aug 29 11:19	Lib Sep 30 18:32
Can Jul 30 19:38	Vir Aug 31 23:27	Sco Oct 03 06:57
Leo Aug 02 05:26	Lib Sep 03 12:29	Sag Oct 05 17:42
Vir Aug 04 17:15	Sco Sep 06 01:08	Cap Oct 08 02:02
Lib Aug 07 06:16	Sag Sep 08 11:53	Aqu Oct 10 07:28
Sco Aug 09 18:49	Cap Sep 10 19:22	Pis Oct 12 09:58

Ari Oct 14 10:24	Gem Nov 14 22:05	Leo Dec 16 17:57
Tau Oct 16 10:16	Can Nov 17 01:33	Vir Dec 19 03:59
Gem Oct 18 11:27	Leo Nov 19 08:38	Lib Dec 21 16:34
Can Oct 20 15:45	Vir Nov 21 19:32	Sco Dec 24 05:06
Leo Oct 23 00:10	Lib Nov 24 08:29	Sag Dec 26 15:06
Vir Oct 25 11:59	Sco Nov 26 20:42	Cap Dec 28 21:47
Lib Oct 28 01:04	Sag Nov 29 06:28	Aqu Dec 31 01:57
Sco Oct 30 13:14	Cap Dec 01 13:37	
Sag Nov 01 23:25	Aqu Dec 03 18:57	**1998**
Cap Nov 04 07:30	Pis Dec 05 23:06	
Aqu Nov 06 13:32	Ari Dec 08 02:23	Pis Jan 02 04:55
Pis Nov 08 17:34	Tau Dec 10 04:59	Ari Jan 04 07:43
Ari Nov 10 19:43	Gem Dec 12 07:35	Tau Jan 06 10:52
Tau Nov 12 20:45	Can Dec 14 11:25	Gem Jan 08 14:42
		Can Jan 10 19:43

Leo Jan 13 02:45	Lib Feb 14 08:17	Sag Mar 18 15:55
Vir Jan 15 12:31	Sco Feb 16 21:12	Cap Mar 21 01:41
Lib Jan 18 00:44	Sag Feb 19 08:55	Aqu Mar 23 08:00
Sco Jan 20 13:33	Cap Feb 21 17:29	Pis Mar 25 10:41
Sag Jan 23 00:23	Aqu Feb 23 22:08	Ari Mar 27 10:48
Cap Jan 25 07:38	Pis Feb 25 23:41	Tau Mar 29 10:06
Aqu Jan 27 11:25	Ari Feb 27 23:42	Gem Mar 31 10:38
Pis Jan 29 13:07	Tau Mar 02 00:01	Can Apr 02 14:10
Ari Jan 31 14:21	Gem Mar 04 02:15	Leo Apr 04 21:36
Tau Feb 02 16:24	Can Mar 06 07:26	Vir Apr 07 08:25
Gem Feb 04 20:09	Leo Mar 08 15:45	Lib Apr 09 21:04
Can Feb 07 01:57	Vir Mar 11 02:35	Sco Apr 12 09:55
Leo Feb 09 09:57	Lib Mar 13 14:57	Sag Apr 14 21:51
Vir Feb 11 20:09	Sco Mar 16 03:50	Cap Apr 17 08:04

Aqu Apr 19 15:40	Ari May 21 06:05	Gem Jun 21 16:26
Pis Apr 21 20:04	Tau May 23 07:05	Can Jun 23 18:38
Ari Apr 23 21:29	Gem May 25 07:25	Leo Jun 25 23:04
Tau Apr 25 21:08	Can May 27 08:59	Vir Jun 28 06:54
Gem Apr 27 20:55	Leo May 29 13:39	Lib Jun 30 18:04
Can Apr 29 22:58	Vir May 31 22:21	Sco Jul 03 06:45
Leo May 02 04:49	Lib Jun 03 10:16	Sag Jul 05 18:23
Vir May 04 14:47	Sco Jun 05 23:04	Cap Jul 08 03:26
Lib May 07 03:18	Sag Jun 08 10:33	Aqu Jul 10 09:51
Sco May 09 16:09	Cap Jun 10 19:49	Pis Jul 12 14:21
Sag May 12 03:47	Aqu Jun 13 03:02	Ari Jul 14 17:44
Cap May 14 13:37	Pis Jun 15 08:30	Tau Jul 16 20:33
Aqu May 16 21:29	Ari Jun 17 12:22	Gem Jul 18 23:18
Pis May 19 03:02	Tau Jun 19 14:47	Can Jul 21 02:43

Leo Jul 23 07:48	Lib Aug 24 10:02	Sag Sep 25 18:04
Vir Jul 25 15:34	Sco Aug 26 22:25	Cap Sep 28 05:29
Lib Jul 28 02:14	Sag Aug 29 10:54	Aqu Sep 30 13:51
Sco Jul 30 14:44	Cap Aug 31 21:21	Pis Oct 02 18:22
Sag Aug 02 02:47	Aqu Sep 03 04:19	Ari Oct 04 19:31
Cap Aug 04 12:16	Pis Sep 05 07:46	Tau Oct 06 18:57
Aqu Aug 06 18:30	Ari Sep 07 08:52	Gem Oct 08 18:43
Pis Aug 08 22:03	Tau Sep 09 09:16	Can Oct 10 20:49
Ari Aug 11 00:09	Gem Sep 11 10:40	Leo Oct 13 02:25
Tau Aug 13 02:04	Can Sep 13 14:20	Vir Oct 15 11:32
Gem Aug 15 04:45	Leo Sep 15 20:48	Lib Oct 17 23:02
Can Aug 17 08:55	Vir Sep 18 05:51	Sco Oct 20 11:36
Leo Aug 19 15:00	Lib Sep 20 16:57	Sag Oct 23 00:15
Vir Aug 21 23:21	Sco Sep 23 05:21	Cap Oct 25 12:03

Aqu Oct 27 21:42	Ari Nov 28 15:32	Gem Dec 30 02:21
Pis Oct 30 03:57	Tau Nov 30 16:51	
Ari Nov 01 06:26	Gem Dec 02 16:29	*1999*
Tau Nov 03 06:11	Can Dec 04 16:27	Can Jan 01 03:15
Gem Nov 05 05:10	Leo Dec 06 18:55	Leo Jan 03 05:30
Can Nov 07 05:39	Vir Dec 09 01:22	Vir Jan 05 10:50
Leo Nov 09 09:33	Lib Dec 11 11:43	Lib Jan 07 19:52
Vir Nov 11 17:36	Sco Dec 14 00:16	Sco Jan 10 07:48
Lib Nov 14 04:57	Sag Dec 16 12:46	Sag Jan 12 20:22
Sco Nov 16 17:40	Cap Dec 18 23:54	Cap Jan 15 07:27
Sag Nov 19 06:12	Aqu Dec 21 09:15	Aqu Jan 17 16:10
Cap Nov 21 17:44	Pis Dec 23 16:44	Pis Jan 19 22:39
Aqu Nov 24 03:42	Ari Dec 25 22:02	Ari Jan 22 03:24
Pis Nov 26 11:12	Tau Dec 28 01:03	Tau Jan 24 06:51

Gem Jan 26 09:28	Leo Feb 26 22:44	Lib Mar 30 20:49
Can Jan 28 11:56	Vir Mar 01 05:04	Sco Apr 02 07:48
Leo Jan 30 15:16	Lib Mar 03 13:34	Sag Apr 04 20:07
Vir Feb 01 20:37	Sco Mar 06 00:22	Cap Apr 07 08:38
Lib Feb 04 04:55	Sag Mar 08 12:45	Aqu Apr 09 19:23
Sco Feb 06 16:06	Cap Mar 11 00:52	Pis Apr 12 02:33
Sag Feb 09 04:37	Aqu Mar 13 10:30	Ari Apr 14 05:45
Cap Feb 11 16:09	Pis Mar 15 16:29	Tau Apr 16 06:06
Aqu Feb 14 00:55	Ari Mar 17 19:12	Gem Apr 18 05:38
Pis Feb 16 06:39	Tau Mar 19 20:08	Can Apr 20 06:27
Ari Feb 18 10:05	Gem Mar 21 21:05	Leo Apr 22 10:06
Tau Feb 20 12:28	Can Mar 23 23:34	Vir Apr 24 17:03
Gem Feb 22 14:53	Leo Mar 26 04:22	Lib Apr 27 02:46
Can Feb 24 18:08	Vir Mar 28 11:34	Sco Apr 29 14:12

Sag May 02 02:35	Aqu Jun 03 08:35	Tau Jul 07 10:20
Cap May 04 15:11	Ari Jun 08 00:06	Gem Jul 09 11:58
Aqu May 07 02:39	Tau Jun 10 02:42	Can Jul 11 12:27
Pis May 09 11:14	Gem Jun 12 02:47	Leo Jul 13 13:26
Ari May 11 15:51	Can Jun 14 02:14	Vir Jul 15 16:38
Tau May 13 16:55	Leo Jun 16 03:07	Lib Jul 17 23:20
Gem May 15 16:07	Vir Jun 18 07:12	Sco Jul 20 09:30
Can May 17 15:39	Lib Jun 20 15:10	Sag Jul 22 21:47
Leo May 19 17:36	Sco Jun 23 02:17	Cap Jul 25 10:07
Vir May 21 23:16	Sag Jun 25 14:50	Aqu Jul 27 20:53
Lib May 24 08:29	Cap Jun 28 03:10	Pis Jul 30 05:26
Sco May 26 20:04	Aqu Jun 30 14:18	Ari Aug 01 11:45
Sag May 29 08:36	Pis Jul 02 23:33	Tau Aug 05 18:56
Cap May 31 21:04	Ari Jul 05 06:20	Can Aug 07 20:52

Leo Aug 09 22:55	Lib Sep 10 17:15	Sag Oct 12 21:18
Vir Aug 12 02:21	Sco Sep 13 02:08	Cap Oct 15 10:02
Lib Aug 14 08:24	Sag Sep 15 13:34	Aqu Oct 17 22:15
Sco Aug 16 17:39	Cap Sep 18 02:12	Pis Oct 20 07:31
Sag Aug 19 05:31	Aqu Sep 20 13:36	Ari Oct 22 12:39
Cap Aug 21 17:59	Pis Sep 22 21:49	Tau Oct 24 14:24
Aqu Aug 24 04:48	Ari Sep 25 02:32	Gem Oct 26 14:33
Pis Aug 26 12:48	Tau Sep 27 04:49	Can Oct 28 15:09
Ari Aug 28 18:08	Gem Sep 29 06:20	Leo Oct 30 17:46
Tau Aug 30 21:39	Can Oct 01 08:31	Vir Nov 01 23:07
Gem Sep 02 00:24	Leo Oct 03 12:13	Lib Nov 04 06:56
Can Sep 04 03:09	Vir Oct 05 17:39	Sco Nov 06 16:45
Leo Sep 06 06:28	Lib Oct 08 00:51	Sag Nov 09 04:14
Vir Sep 08 10:56	Sco Oct 10 10:01	Cap Nov 11 16:59

Aqu Nov 14 05:44	Ari Dec 16 07:28	Ari Jan 12 13:46
Pis Nov 16 16:19	Tau Dec 18 11:43	Tau Jan 14 19:36
Ari Nov 18 22:55	Gem Dec 20 12:37	Gem Jan 16 22:23
Tau Nov 21 01:24	Can Dec 22 11:52	Can Jan 18 23:00
Gem Nov 23 01:13	Leo Dec 24 11:32	Leo Jan 20 22:58
Can Nov 25 00:29	Vir Dec 26 13:34	Vir Jan 23 00:07
Leo Nov 27 01:19	Lib Dec 28 19:14	Lib Jan 25 04:09
Vir Nov 29 05:10	Sco Dec 31 04:36	Sco Jan 27 12:01
Lib Dec 01 12:29		Sag Jan 29 23:17
Sco Dec 03 22:35	**2000**	Cap Feb 01 12:09
Sag Dec 06 10:27	Sag Jan 02 16:31	Aqu Feb 04 00:30
Cap Dec 08 23:12	Cap Jan 05 05:23	Pis Feb 06 11:00
Aqu Dec 11 11:57	Aqu Jan 07 17:52	Ari Feb 08 19:16
Pis Dec 13 23:15	Pis Jan 10 04:58	Tau Feb 11 01:19

Gem Feb 13 05:22	Leo Mar 15 16:42	Lib Apr 16 07:35
Can Feb 15 07:44	Vir Mar 17 19:48	Sco Apr 18 14:35
Leo Feb 17 09:11	Lib Mar 19 23:57	Sag Apr 20 23:57
Vir Feb 19 10:53	Sco Mar 22 06:17	Cap Apr 23 11:46
Lib Feb 21 14:21	Sag Mar 24 15:42	Aqu Apr 26 00:40
Sco Feb 23 20:58	Cap Mar 27 03:50	Pis Apr 28 12:04
Sag Feb 26 07:09	Aqu Mar 29 16:33	Ari Apr 30 19:53
Cap Feb 28 19:44	Pis Apr 01 03:10	Tau May 02 23:52
Aqu Mar 02 08:13	Ari Apr 03 10:20	Gem May 05 01:22
Pis Mar 04 18:29	Tau Apr 05 14:27	Can May 07 02:13
Ari Mar 07 01:52	Gem Apr 07 16:57	Leo May 09 04:01
Tau Mar 09 07:00	Can Apr 09 19:15	Vir May 11 07:40
Gem Mar 11 10:44	Leo Apr 11 22:15	Lib May 13 13:27
Can Mar 13 13:50	Vir Apr 14 02:18	Sco May 15 21:16

Sag May 18 07:09	Aqu Jun 19 14:25	Ari Jul 21 19:08
Cap May 20 19:00	Pis Jun 22 02:50	Tau Jul 24 02:42
Aqu May 23 07:59	Ari Jun 24 12:53	Gem Jul 26 07:00
Pis May 25 20:06	Tau Jun 26 19:17	Can Jul 28 08:28
Ari May 28 05:06	Gem Jun 28 21:57	Leo Jul 30 08:23
Tau May 30 10:00	Can Jun 30 22:08	Vir Aug 01 08:27
Gem Jun 01 11:33	Leo Jul 02 21:37	Lib Aug 03 10:32
Can Jun 03 11:29	Vir Jul 04 22:19	Sco Aug 05 16:04
Leo Jun 05 11:45	Lib Jul 07 01:47	Sag Aug 08 01:30
Vir Jun 07 13:57	Sco Jul 09 08:48	Cap Aug 10 13:43
Lib Jun 09 18:58	Sag Jul 11 19:05	Aqu Aug 13 02:42
Sco Jun 12 02:55	Cap Jul 14 07:27	Pis Aug 15 14:40
Sag Jun 14 13:18	Aqu Jul 16 20:25	Ari Aug 18 00:42
Cap Jun 17 01:26	Pis Jul 19 08:42	Tau Aug 20 08:29

Gem Aug 22 13:53	Leo Sep 23 01:59	Lib Oct 24 14:29
Can Aug 24 16:58	Vir Sep 25 04:01	Sco Oct 26 19:23
Leo Aug 26 18:16	Lib Sep 27 06:21	Sag Oct 29 02:40
Vir Aug 28 18:54	Sco Sep 29 10:30	Cap Oct 31 13:01
Lib Aug 30 20:33	Sag Oct 01 17:49	Aqu Nov 03 01:39
Sco Sep 02 00:56	Cap Oct 04 04:42	Pis Nov 05 14:11
Sag Sep 04 09:08	Aqu Oct 06 17:32	Ari Nov 08 00:00
Cap Sep 06 20:46	Pis Oct 09 05:35	Tau Nov 10 06:11
Aqu Sep 09 09:43	Ari Oct 11 14:49	Gem Nov 12 09:26
Pis Sep 11 21:32	Tau Oct 13 21:04	Can Nov 14 11:20
Ari Sep 14 06:59	Gem Oct 16 01:17	Leo Nov 16 13:18
Tau Sep 16 14:04	Can Oct 18 04:36	Vir Nov 18 16:15
Gem Sep 18 19:21	Leo Oct 20 07:41	Lib Nov 20 20:34
Can Sep 20 23:14	Vir Oct 22 10:52	Sco Nov 23 02:32

Sag Nov 25 10:32	Aqu Dec 27 16:24	Aqu Jan 23 22:42
Cap Nov 27 20:56	Pis Dec 30 05:26	Pis Jan 26 11:37
Aqu Nov 30 09:25		Ari Jan 28 23:33
Pis Dec 02 22:21	**2001**	Tau Jan 31 09:19
Ari Dec 05 09:15	Ari Jan 01 17:13	Gem Feb 02 15:54
Tau Dec 07 16:25	Tau Jan 04 01:54	Can Feb 04 18:59
Gem Dec 09 19:49	Gem Jan 06 06:43	Leo Feb 06 19:20
Can Dec 11 20:47	Can Jan 08 08:07	Vir Feb 08 18:34
Leo Dec 13 21:08	Leo Jan 10 07:43	Lib Feb 10 18:45
Vir Dec 15 22:30	Vir Jan 12 07:25	Sco Feb 12 21:52
Lib Dec 18 02:01	Lib Jan 14 09:05	Sag Feb 15 05:02
Sco Dec 20 08:11	Sco Jan 16 14:03	Cap Feb 17 15:58
Sag Dec 22 16:56	Sag Jan 18 22:36	Aqu Feb 20 04:53
Cap Dec 25 03:53	Cap Jan 21 09:56	Pis Feb 22 17:44

Ari Feb 25 05:19	Gem Mar 29 04:00	Leo Apr 29 18:24
Tau Feb 27 15:04	Can Mar 31 09:21	Vir May 01 21:15
Gem Mar 01 22:34	Leo Apr 02 12:52	Lib May 03 23:49
Can Mar 04 03:23	Vir Apr 04 14:45	Sco May 06 03:00
Leo Mar 06 05:29	Lib Apr 06 15:56	Sag May 08 08:05
Vir Mar 08 05:43	Sco Apr 08 18:00	Cap May 10 16:09
Lib Mar 10 05:46	Sag Apr 10 22:47	Aqu May 13 03:19
Sco Mar 12 07:42	Cap Apr 13 07:20	Pis May 15 16:00
Sag Mar 14 13:17	Aqu Apr 15 19:10	Ari May 18 03:39
Cap Mar 16 23:02	Pis Apr 18 07:59	Tau May 20 12:27
Aqu Mar 19 11:35	Ari Apr 20 19:16	Gem May 22 18:11
Pis Mar 22 00:27	Tau Apr 23 03:54	Can May 24 21:41
Ari Mar 24 11:42	Gem Apr 25 10:10	Leo May 27 00:11
Tau Mar 26 20:49	Can Apr 27 14:48	Vir May 29 02:37

Lib May 31 05:40	Sag Jul 01 22:13	Aqu Aug 03 00:52
Sco Jun 02 09:56	Cap Jul 04 07:21	Pis Aug 05 13:29
Sag Jun 04 15:57	Aqu Jul 06 18:32	Ari Aug 08 02:03
Cap Jun 07 00:23	Pis Jul 09 07:04	Tau Aug 10 13:21
Aqu Jun 09 11:19	Ari Jul 11 19:34	Gem Aug 12 21:56
Pis Jun 11 23:52	Tau Jul 14 06:12	Can Aug 15 02:53
Ari Jun 14 12:01	Gem Jul 16 13:23	Leo Aug 17 04:24
Tau Jun 16 21:37	Can Jul 18 16:55	Vir Aug 19 03:52
Gem Jun 19 03:40	Leo Jul 20 17:42	Lib Aug 21 03:18
Can Jun 21 06:40	Vir Jul 22 17:28	Sco Aug 23 04:49
Leo Jun 23 07:54	Lib Jul 24 18:07	Sag Aug 25 09:59
Vir Jun 25 08:57	Sco Jul 26 21:17	Cap Aug 27 19:01
Lib Jun 27 11:10	Sag Jul 29 03:44	Aqu Aug 30 06:46
Sco Jun 29 15:28	Cap Jul 31 13:16	Pis Sep 01 19:31

Ari Sep 04 07:57	Gem Oct 06 10:10	Leo Nov 07 03:32
Tau Sep 06 19:16	Can Oct 08 17:18	Vir Nov 09 06:48
Gem Sep 09 04:39	Leo Oct 10 21:52	Lib Nov 11 08:52
Can Sep 11 11:07	Vir Oct 12 23:56	Sco Nov 13 10:44
Leo Sep 13 14:14	Lib Oct 15 00:25	Sag Nov 15 13:51
Vir Sep 15 14:38	Sco Oct 17 01:02	Cap Nov 17 19:39
Lib Sep 17 13:59	Sag Oct 19 03:47	Aqu Nov 20 04:54
Sco Sep 19 14:27	Cap Oct 21 10:12	Pis Nov 22 16:51
Sag Sep 21 18:01	Aqu Oct 23 20:26	Ari Nov 25 05:20
Cap Sep 24 01:48	Pis Oct 26 08:54	Tau Nov 27 16:04
Aqu Sep 26 13:04	Ari Oct 28 21:13	Gem Nov 30 00:02
Pis Sep 29 01:49	Tau Oct 31 07:46	Can Dec 02 05:29
Ari Oct 01 14:06	Gem Nov 02 16:11	Leo Dec 04 09:14
Tau Oct 04 00:59	Can Nov 04 22:42	Vir Dec 06 12:10

Lib Dec 08 14:56	Lib Jan 04 20:23	Sag Feb 05 10:21
Sco Dec 10 18:08	Sco Jan 06 23:41	Cap Feb 07 18:07
Sag Dec 12 22:29	Sag Jan 09 04:57	Aqu Feb 10 04:14
Cap Dec 15 04:47	Cap Jan 11 12:18	Pis Feb 12 15:52
Aqu Dec 17 13:43	Aqu Jan 13 21:41	Ari Feb 15 04:24
Pis Dec 20 01:09	Pis Jan 16 08:59	Tau Feb 17 16:57
Ari Dec 22 13:44	Ari Jan 18 21:34	Gem Feb 20 03:48
Tau Dec 25 01:10	Tau Jan 21 09:45	Can Feb 22 11:13
Gem Dec 27 09:37	Gem Jan 23 19:26	Leo Feb 24 14:34
Can Dec 29 14:38	Can Jan 26 01:15	Vir Feb 26 14:45
Leo Dec 31 17:08	Leo Jan 28 03:29	Lib Feb 28 13:46
	Vir Jan 30 03:39	Sco Mar 02 13:52
2002	Lib Feb 01 03:44	Sag Mar 04 16:54
Vir Jan 02 18:33	Sco Feb 03 05:34	Cap Mar 06 23:48

356

Aqu Mar 09 09:56	Ari Apr 10 16:39	Gem May 12 22:03
Pis Mar 11 21:56	Tau Apr 13 04:54	Can May 15 06:32
Ari Mar 14 10:33	Gem Apr 15 15:55	Leo May 17 12:50
Tau Mar 16 22:59	Can Apr 18 00:59	Vir May 19 16:59
Gem Mar 19 10:18	Leo Apr 20 07:19	Lib May 21 19:17
Can Mar 21 19:05	Vir Apr 22 10:33	Sco May 23 20:37
Leo Mar 24 00:10	Lib Apr 24 11:20	Sag May 25 22:19
Vir Mar 26 01:42	Sco Apr 26 11:15	Cap May 28 01:54
Lib Mar 28 01:03	Sag Apr 28 12:13	Aqu May 30 08:34
Sco Mar 30 00:21	Cap Apr 30 16:02	Pis Jun 01 18:36
Sag Apr 01 01:49	Aqu May 02 23:44	Ari Jun 04 06:50
Cap Apr 03 06:58	Pis May 05 10:45	Tau Jun 06 19:05
Aqu Apr 05 16:06	Ari May 07 23:21	Gem Jun 09 05:28
Pis Apr 08 03:57	Tau May 10 11:30	Can Jun 11 13:13

Leo Jun 13 18:38	Lib Jul 15 06:38	Sag Aug 15 18:24
Vir Jun 15 22:22	Sco Jul 17 09:12	Cap Aug 18 00:15
Lib Jun 18 01:10	Sag Jul 19 13:02	Aqu Aug 20 08:16
Sco Jun 20 03:41	Cap Jul 21 18:25	Pis Aug 22 18:10
Sag Jun 22 06:41	Aqu Jul 24 01:39	Ari Aug 25 05:46
Cap Jun 24 11:01	Pis Jul 26 11:04	Tau Aug 27 18:30
Aqu Jun 26 17:35	Ari Jul 28 22:38	Gem Aug 30 06:44
Pis Jun 29 03:00	Tau Jul 31 11:15	Can Sep 01 16:12
Ari Jul 01 14:48	Gem Aug 02 22:44	Leo Sep 03 21:34
Tau Jul 04 03:15	Can Aug 05 07:00	Vir Sep 05 23:14
Gem Jul 06 13:58	Leo Aug 07 11:25	Lib Sep 07 22:56
Can Jul 08 21:34	Vir Aug 09 13:02	Sco Sep 09 22:48
Leo Jul 11 02:06	Lib Aug 11 13:37	Sag Sep 12 00:44
Vir Jul 13 04:39	Sco Aug 13 15:00	Cap Sep 14 05:47

Aqu Sep 16 13:54	Ari Oct 18 18:12	Gem Nov 20 01:23
Pis Sep 19 00:17	Tau Oct 21 06:55	Can Nov 22 11:46
Ari Sep 21 12:10	Gem Oct 23 19:16	Leo Nov 24 19:58
Tau Sep 24 00:53	Can Oct 26 06:09	Vir Nov 27 01:40
Gem Sep 26 13:25	Leo Oct 28 14:18	Lib Nov 29 04:53
Can Sep 28 23:59	Vir Oct 30 18:58	Sco Dec 01 06:14
Leo Oct 01 06:57	Lib Nov 01 20:27	Sag Dec 03 06:57
Vir Oct 03 09:50	Sco Nov 03 20:09	Cap Dec 05 08:38
Lib Oct 05 09:50	Sag Nov 05 20:01	Aqu Dec 07 12:54
Sco Oct 07 08:57	Cap Nov 07 21:59	Pis Dec 09 20:46
Sag Oct 09 09:21	Aqu Nov 10 03:27	Ari Dec 12 07:57
Cap Oct 11 12:45	Pis Nov 12 12:41	Tau Dec 14 20:42
Aqu Oct 13 19:51	Ari Nov 15 00:37	Gem Dec 17 08:41
Pis Oct 16 06:06	Tau Nov 17 13:22	Can Dec 19 18:29

Leo Dec 22 01:47	Leo Jan 18 09:27	Lib Feb 18 23:47
Vir Dec 24 07:04	Vir Jan 20 13:30	Sco Feb 21 01:09
Lib Dec 26 10:52	Lib Jan 22 16:22	Sag Feb 23 03:45
Sco Dec 28 13:40	Sco Jan 24 19:08	Cap Feb 25 08:10
Sag Dec 30 16:00	Sag Jan 26 22:25	Aqu Feb 27 14:24
	Cap Jan 29 02:29	Pis Mar 01 22:25
2003	Aqu Jan 31 07:44	Ari Mar 04 08:29
Cap Jan 01 18:42	Pis Feb 02 14:54	Tau Mar 06 20:35
Aqu Jan 03 22:57	Ari Feb 05 00:44	Gem Mar 09 09:36
Pis Jan 06 05:56	Tau Feb 07 12:58	Can Mar 11 21:10
Ari Jan 08 16:14	Gem Feb 10 01:44	Leo Mar 14 05:05
Tau Jan 11 04:47	Can Feb 12 12:17	Vir Mar 16 08:51
Gem Jan 13 17:06	Leo Feb 14 19:03	Lib Mar 18 09:42
Can Jan 16 02:54	Vir Feb 16 22:21	Sco Mar 20 09:37

Sag Mar 22 10:33	Aqu Apr 23 01:58	Ari May 25 02:58
Cap Mar 24 13:48	Pis Apr 25 10:02	Tau May 27 15:31
Aqu Mar 26 19:50	Ari Apr 27 20:54	Gem May 30 04:30
Pis Mar 29 04:25	Tau Apr 30 09:25	Can Jun 01 16:26
Ari Mar 31 15:04	Gem May 02 22:26	Leo Jun 04 02:23
Tau Apr 03 03:19	Can May 05 10:40	Vir Jun 06 09:49
Gem Apr 05 16:23	Leo May 07 20:44	Lib Jun 08 14:28
Can Apr 08 04:35	Vir May 10 03:29	Sco Jun 10 16:37
Leo Apr 10 13:51	Lib May 12 06:41	Sag Jun 12 17:11
Vir Apr 12 19:05	Sco May 14 07:12	Cap Jun 14 17:37
Lib Apr 14 20:40	Sag May 16 06:42	Aqu Jun 16 19:41
Sco Apr 16 20:15	Cap May 18 07:03	Pis Jun 19 00:57
Sag Apr 18 19:51	Aqu May 20 10:01	Ari Jun 21 10:05
Cap Apr 20 21:20	Pis May 22 16:40	Tau Jun 23 22:14

Gem Jun 26 11:11	Leo Jul 28 15:15	Lib Aug 29 08:40
Can Jun 28 22:50	Vir Jul 30 21:25	Sco Aug 31 10:59
Leo Jul 01 08:12	Lib Aug 02 01:46	Sag Sep 02 13:31
Vir Jul 03 15:14	Sco Aug 04 05:11	Cap Sep 04 16:50
Lib Jul 05 20:19	Sag Aug 06 08:10	Aqu Sep 06 21:14
Sco Jul 07 23:42	Cap Aug 08 11:02	Pis Sep 09 03:06
Sag Jul 10 01:47	Aqu Aug 10 14:23	Ari Sep 11 11:09
Cap Jul 12 03:20	Pis Aug 12 19:18	Tau Sep 13 21:49
Aqu Jul 14 05:37	Ari Aug 15 03:00	Gem Sep 16 10:31
Pis Jul 16 10:14	Tau Aug 17 13:52	Can Sep 18 23:06
Ari Jul 18 18:18	Gem Aug 20 02:40	Leo Sep 21 09:01
Tau Jul 21 05:47	Can Aug 22 14:43	Vir Sep 23 15:02
Gem Jul 23 18:41	Leo Aug 24 23:46	Lib Sep 25 17:48
Can Jul 26 06:22	Vir Aug 27 05:25	Sco Sep 27 18:51

Sag Sep 29 19:56	Aqu Oct 31 08:41	Ari Dec 02 05:55
Cap Oct 01 22:21	Pis Nov 02 14:52	Tau Dec 04 17:29
Aqu Oct 04 02:45	Ari Nov 05 00:02	Gem Dec 07 06:25
Pis Oct 06 09:20	Tau Nov 07 11:28	Can Dec 09 19:10
Ari Oct 08 18:07	Gem Nov 10 00:13	Leo Dec 12 06:39
Tau Oct 11 05:04	Can Nov 12 13:09	Vir Dec 14 16:05
Gem Oct 13 17:44	Leo Nov 15 00:46	Lib Dec 16 22:44
Can Oct 16 06:40	Vir Nov 17 09:34	Sco Dec 19 02:18
Leo Oct 18 17:40	Lib Nov 19 14:40	Sag Dec 21 03:14
Vir Oct 21 00:59	Sco Nov 21 16:22	Cap Dec 23 02:55
Lib Oct 23 04:25	Sag Nov 23 16:02	Aqu Dec 25 03:13
Sco Oct 25 05:07	Cap Nov 25 15:31	Pis Dec 27 06:09
Sag Oct 27 04:54	Aqu Nov 27 16:48	Ari Dec 29 13:09
Cap Oct 29 05:36	Pis Nov 29 21:26	

2004

Tau Jan 01 00:01	Gem Jan 30 20:17	Leo Mar 03 04:16
Gem Jan 03 12:57	Can Feb 02 09:02	Vir Mar 05 12:16
Can Jan 06 01:37	Leo Feb 04 19:49	Lib Mar 07 17:30
Leo Jan 08 12:37	Vir Feb 07 04:01	Sco Mar 09 21:02
Vir Jan 10 21:36	Lib Feb 09 10:11	Sag Mar 11 23:56
Lib Jan 13 04:37	Sco Feb 11 14:56	Cap Mar 14 02:51
Sco Jan 15 09:31	Sag Feb 13 18:34	Aqu Mar 16 06:09
Sag Jan 17 12:16	Cap Feb 15 21:13	Pis Mar 18 10:26
Cap Jan 19 13:23	Aqu Feb 17 23:27	Ari Mar 20 16:28
Aqu Jan 21 14:10	Pis Feb 20 02:27	Tau Mar 23 01:09
Pis Jan 23 16:28	Ari Feb 22 07:45	Gem Mar 25 12:34
Ari Jan 25 22:06	Tau Feb 24 16:30	Can Mar 28 01:22
Tau Jan 28 07:46	Gem Feb 27 04:22	Leo Mar 30 13:05
	Can Feb 29 17:11	Vir Apr 01 21:43

Lib Apr 04 02:50	Sag May 05 16:07	Aqu Jun 06 02:10
Sco Apr 06 05:23	Cap May 07 16:16	Pis Jun 08 04:38
Sag Apr 08 06:49	Aqu May 09 17:45	Ari Jun 10 10:50
Cap Apr 10 08:33	Pis May 11 21:52	Tau Jun 12 20:36
Aqu Apr 12 11:33	Ari May 14 05:02	Gem Jun 15 08:43
Pis Apr 14 16:23	Tau May 16 14:56	Can Jun 17 21:36
Ari Apr 16 23:24	Gem May 19 02:46	Leo Jun 20 10:03
Tau Apr 19 08:42	Can May 21 15:34	Vir Jun 22 21:08
Gem Apr 21 20:09	Leo May 24 04:06	Lib Jun 25 05:49
Can Apr 24 08:55	Vir May 26 14:50	Sco Jun 27 11:10
Leo Apr 26 21:13	Lib May 28 22:20	Sag Jun 29 13:14
Vir Apr 29 06:59	Sco May 31 02:06	Cap Jul 01 13:00
Lib May 01 13:00	Sag Jun 02 02:51	Aqu Jul 03 12:22
Sco May 03 15:37	Cap Jun 04 02:12	Pis Jul 05 13:27

Ari Jul 07 18:02	Gem Aug 08 21:32	Leo Sep 10 06:05
Tau Jul 10 02:50	Can Aug 11 10:19	Vir Sep 12 16:15
Gem Jul 12 14:44	Leo Aug 13 22:28	Lib Sep 14 23:52
Can Jul 15 03:40	Vir Aug 16 08:48	Sco Sep 17 05:24
Leo Jul 17 15:55	Lib Aug 18 17:08	Sag Sep 19 09:28
Vir Jul 20 02:43	Sco Aug 20 23:35	Cap Sep 21 12:34
Lib Jul 22 11:37	Sag Aug 23 04:07	Aqu Sep 23 15:09
Sco Jul 24 18:07	Cap Aug 25 06:46	Pis Sep 25 17:55
Sag Jul 26 21:46	Aqu Aug 27 08:07	Ari Sep 27 21:57
Cap Jul 28 22:56	Pis Aug 29 09:33	Tau Sep 30 04:23
Aqu Jul 30 22:54	Ari Aug 31 12:46	Gem Oct 02 13:55
Pis Aug 01 23:35	Tau Sep 02 19:15	Can Oct 05 01:53
Ari Aug 04 03:00	Gem Sep 05 05:24	Leo Oct 07 14:22
Tau Aug 06 10:26	Can Sep 07 17:49	Vir Oct 10 00:58

Lib Oct 12 08:30	Sag Nov 13 00:55	Aqu Dec 14 11:10
Sco Oct 14 13:09	Cap Nov 15 01:32	Pis Dec 16 12:24
Sag Oct 16 15:57	Aqu Nov 17 02:39	Ari Dec 18 16:52
Cap Oct 18 18:06	Pis Nov 19 05:37	Tau Dec 21 00:52
Aqu Oct 20 20:37	Ari Nov 21 11:11	Gem Dec 23 11:32
Pis Oct 23 00:13	Tau Nov 23 19:15	Can Dec 25 23:37
Ari Oct 25 05:24	Gem Nov 26 05:24	Leo Dec 28 12:13
Tau Oct 27 12:37	Can Nov 28 17:10	Vir Dec 31 00:32
Gem Oct 29 22:11	Leo Dec 01 05:49	
Can Nov 01 09:52	Vir Dec 03 17:59	*2005*
Leo Nov 03 22:31	Lib Dec 06 03:45	Lib Jan 02 11:18
Vir Nov 06 09:58	Sco Dec 08 09:41	Sco Jan 04 18:58
Lib Nov 08 18:22	Sag Dec 10 11:52	Sag Jan 06 22:42
Sco Nov 10 23:03	Cap Dec 12 11:41	Cap Jan 08 23:09

Aqu Jan 10 22:07	Ari Feb 11 10:22	Gem Mar 15 08:44
Pis Jan 12 21:51	Tau Feb 13 15:18	Can Mar 17 19:43
Ari Jan 15 00:27	Gem Feb 16 00:18	Leo Mar 20 08:16
Tau Jan 17 07:06	Can Feb 18 12:12	Vir Mar 22 20:09
Gem Jan 19 17:23	Leo Feb 21 00:53	Lib Mar 25 05:59
Can Jan 22 05:41	Vir Feb 23 12:43	Sco Mar 27 13:27
Leo Jan 24 18:20	Lib Feb 25 22:57	Sag Mar 29 18:55
Vir Jan 27 06:23	Sco Feb 28 07:19	Cap Mar 31 22:47
Lib Jan 29 17:12	Sag Mar 02 13:28	Aqu Apr 03 01:30
Sco Feb 01 01:49	Cap Mar 04 17:11	Pis Apr 05 03:45
Sag Feb 03 07:20	Aqu Mar 06 18:48	Ari Apr 07 06:27
Cap Feb 05 09:30	Pis Mar 08 19:32	Tau Apr 09 10:50
Aqu Feb 07 09:25	Ari Mar 10 21:03	Gem Apr 11 17:54
Pis Feb 09 08:59	Tau Mar 13 01:06	Can Apr 14 04:03

Leo Apr 16 16:16	Lib May 18 23:28	Sag Jun 19 20:43
Vir Apr 19 04:26	Sco May 21 06:47	Cap Jun 21 21:51
Lib Apr 21 14:25	Sag May 23 10:36	Aqu Jun 23 21:36
Sco Apr 23 21:24	Cap May 25 12:10	Pis Jun 25 22:03
Sag Apr 26 01:44	Aqu May 27 13:09	Ari Jun 28 00:52
Cap Apr 28 04:32	Pis May 29 15:09	Tau Jun 30 06:44
Aqu Apr 30 06:53	Ari May 31 19:07	Gem Jul 02 15:25
Pis May 02 09:42	Tau Jun 03 01:19	Can Jul 05 02:07
Ari May 04 13:36	Gem Jun 05 09:35	Leo Jul 07 14:10
Tau May 06 19:01	Can Jun 07 19:46	Vir Jul 10 02:56
Gem May 09 02:28	Leo Jun 10 07:39	Lib Jul 12 15:08
Can May 11 12:20	Vir Jun 12 20:21	Sco Jul 15 00:49
Leo May 14 00:16	Lib Jun 15 07:57	Sag Jul 17 06:34
Vir May 16 12:45	Sco Jun 17 16:22	Cap Jul 19 08:25

Aqu Jul 21 07:54	Ari Aug 21 18:00	Gem Sep 22 12:07
Pis Jul 23 07:11	Tau Aug 23 20:58	Can Sep 24 21:10
Ari Jul 25 08:23	Gem Aug 26 03:43	Leo Sep 27 09:02
Tau Jul 27 12:55	Can Aug 28 13:57	Vir Sep 29 21:43
Gem Jul 29 21:02	Leo Aug 31 02:14	Lib Oct 02 09:23
Can Aug 01 07:52	Vir Sep 02 14:55	Sco Oct 04 19:02
Leo Aug 03 20:09	Lib Sep 05 02:51	Sag Oct 07 02:27
Vir Aug 06 08:53	Sco Sep 07 13:09	Cap Oct 09 07:42
Lib Aug 08 21:07	Sag Sep 09 21:01	Aqu Oct 11 11:04
Sco Aug 11 07:33	Cap Sep 12 01:55	Pis Oct 13 13:04
Sag Aug 13 14:45	Aqu Sep 14 04:01	Ari Oct 15 14:39
Cap Aug 15 18:12	Pis Sep 16 04:24	Tau Oct 17 17:04
Aqu Aug 17 18:38	Ari Sep 18 04:42	Gem Oct 19 21:44
Pis Aug 19 17:52	Tau Sep 20 06:47	Can Oct 22 05:40

Leo Oct 24 16:48	Lib Nov 26 01:56	Sag Dec 28 03:42
Vir Oct 27 05:27	Sco Nov 28 11:31	Cap Dec 30 06:34
Lib Oct 29 17:14	Sag Nov 30 17:31	
Sco Nov 01 02:27	Cap Dec 02 20:41	
Sag Nov 03 08:54	Aqu Dec 04 22:36	
Cap Nov 05 13:16	Pis Dec 07 00:44	
Aqu Nov 07 16:30	Ari Dec 09 04:02	
Pis Nov 09 19:22	Tau Dec 11 08:46	
Ari Nov 11 22:22	Gem Dec 13 14:59	
Tau Nov 14 02:02	Can Dec 15 23:01	
Gem Nov 16 07:09	Leo Dec 18 09:18	
Can Nov 18 14:42	Vir Dec 20 21:38	
Leo Nov 21 01:10	Lib Dec 23 10:25	
Vir Nov 23 13:41	Sco Dec 25 21:02	

This book was

typeset in Centaur and KuenstlerScript
by Nina Gaskin.

Book design by

Judith Stagnitto Abbate and Junie Lee